THE SAMUEL & ALTHEA STROUM
LECTURES IN JEWISH STUDIES

S AMUEL STROUM, businessman, community leader, and philanthropist, by a major gift to the Jewish Federation of Greater Seattle, established the Samuel and Althea Stroum Philanthropic Fund.

In recognition of Mr. and Mrs. Stroum's deep interest in Jewish history and culture, the Board of Directors of the Jewish Federation of Greater Seattle, in cooperation with the Jewish Studies Program at the University of Washington, established an annual lectureship at the University of Washington known as the Samuel and Althea Stroum Lectureship in Jewish Studies. This lectureship makes it possible to bring to the area outstanding scholars and interpreters of Jewish thought, thus promoting a deeper understanding of Jewish history, religion, and culture. Such understanding can lead to an enhanced appreciation of the Jewish contributions to the historical and cultural traditions that have shaped the American nation.

The terms of the gift also provide for the publication from time to time of the lectures or other appropriate materials resulting from or related to the lectures. A complete list of the books in the series appears at the end of this book.

Writing in Tongues

TRANSLATING YIDDISH IN THE TWENTIETH CENTURY

Anita Norich

A Samuel and Althea Stroum Book

UNIVERSITY OF WASHINGTON PRESS
Seattle and London

© 2013 by the University of Washington Press
Printed and bound in the United States of America
18 17 16 15 14 13   5 4 3 2 1

This book is published with the assistance of a grant from the Samuel
and Althea Stroum Endowed Book Fund.

University of Washington Press
PO Box 50096, Seattle, WA 98145, USA
www.washington.edu/uwpress

Library of Congress Cataloging-in-Publication Data
Norich, Anita, 1952–
Writing in Tongues : translating Yiddish in the twentieth century /
Anita Norich. — First edition.
    pages cm — (Samuel and Althea Stroum lectures in Jewish studies)
ISBN 978-0-295-99296-9 (cloth) — ISBN 978-0-295-99297-6 (paperback)
1. Yiddish literature—Translating. 2. Yiddish language—Translating.
3. Yiddish literature—History and criticism. I. Title.
PJ5120.5.N67 2013   439'.1802—dc23   2013026551

The paper used in this publication is acid-free and meets the minimum requirements
of American National Standard for Information Sciences—Permanence of Paper for
Printed Library Materials, ANSI Z39.48–1984.∞

Lovingly dedicated to Sara Taibl Norich

What is translation? On a platter
A poet's pale and glaring head,
A parrot's screech, a monkey's chatter,
And profanation of the dead.
. . . .
This is my task—a poet's patience
And scholastic passion blent:
Dove-droppings on your monument.
—Vladimir Nabokov, "On Translating 'Eugene Onegin'"

Contents

Preface   ix

Acknowledgments   xiii

CHAPTER 1

Translation Theory and Practice: The Yiddish Difference   3

CHAPTER 2

How Tevye Learned to Fiddle   22

CHAPTER 3

Remembering Jews: Translating Yiddish after the Holocaust   42

CHAPTER 4

Returning to and from the Ghetto: Yankev Glatshteyn   66

CHAPTER 5

Concluding Lines and Conclusions   97

APPENDIX A

Anna Margolin's "Maris tfile" in Yiddish and Translations   109

APPENDIX B

Twelve Translations of Yankev Glatshteyn's "A gute nakht, velt"   113

Notes   129

Bibliography   147

Index   157

Preface

אָ, לאָזט מיך צו צו דער פֿרייד פֿון ייִדישן װאָרט.

O, lozt mikh tsu tsu der freyd fun yidishn vort.
Oh, let me through/in/get near to the joy of the Yiddish word.
> —Yankev Glatshteyn, *Di freyd fun yidishn vort*
> (The joy of the Yiddish word)

ONE day, soon after my family arrived in the United States, we ventured forth to find the Bronx. We were going to visit friends my parents had known in Poland and Germany, with whom they had endured a ghetto and several concentration camps and whom they had not seen in almost a decade. I knew, as only a four-year-old can know such things, that this was an epic moment, one marking a definitive transition in both location and language. En route, I was reassured that these friends had two daughters who would be friendly. Finally, there would be kids I could play with.

All I had to do, my father explained in my native Yiddish, was to say that magical English word, "hello." The children would reply with "hello" and I could start my happy new life in the new land. As we sat on the straw-woven seats of the IRT #4 train, I practiced and practiced. I was comforted by my ability to use it flawlessly. "Hello" was more promising than the subway itself, more interesting than the machines that would have given us chewing gum if only I had had a penny (or known what chewing gum was), and certainly more hopeful than the dirt and noise that surrounded us. My rapture, my delight, my anxiety, I later learned, were the tropes of the immigrant experience, mere clichés, although certainly not for me there and then.

We arrived. I saw two girls, a few years older than I. As our parents embraced, I went over to the younger of the two girls.

"Hello," I said, with all the enthusiasm my new American self could muster.

She replied, equally enthusiastic: "Hi!"

And I flung myself onto the couch and burst into tears, overcome by frustration and fear.

Almost twenty-five years later, I am in Jerusalem, studying at the Hebrew University. I confidently approach the guard who checks through our bags each morning. I wait in line to wish him a flawless "good morning." I say "*boker tov*" in what I take to be a perfect accent, certain that he will not detect that this is merely my second day of studying Hebrew, and hoping he won't ask me anything or try to strike up a conversation. He replies with a friendly "*boker or*," and I am, once again, a panicked four-year-old, once again uncomprehending and incomprehensible.

Why does anyone need "hi" when they have "hello"? Why do people say "*boker or*" when "*boker tov*" is what's in all the dictionaries? And how am I supposed to know when to use one instead of the other? The English-learning child I was could not begin to understand the verbal betrayal that had just occurred; my Hebrew-learning academic self wanted to know if one phrase was more informal than the other, or more polite, or what nuanced difference they indicate. Each time, just as in innumerable other moments in all of our complex lingual lives, I translated my Yiddish "*sholem aleykhem*" or "*gut morgn*" perfectly, and yet I *still* did not get it right. The shock of these moments has remained with me and led me, through various circuitous routes, to this study. It has led to different questions, but one remains: what does it mean to "get it right"?

*   *   *

By strict linguistic standards, my parents never got it quite right. Their English remained marked by their distinct accents and by their sometimes hypercorrect, sometimes simply incorrect, renditions of fluent English speech and writing. But they always got it. I learned from them, among so many other things, the intelligence behind what I once took to be errors, and the necessity of translating from what is native to what is strange, both the estrangement in that act and the power it conveys. I learned that what might be dismissed by some as a mistake can contain emotional, political, and intellectual profundity, that there is no tension between malapropism and dignity, that the halting can be graceful. I learned to pay attention to word choice and sentence construction, to the Yiddish in their English and the English itself. (Naively, I never thought of their Yiddish as constructed but rather as something that simply was.) This book is theirs. They would have read it in any language and translated it into the language of pride and love.

When I was young I used to imagine having so many children that I could name one after all the people my parents had mourned after World War II. Years later, I tried to imagine writing many books so I could dedicate one to each of those people. Neither fantasy could ever have come true. Instead, I often find myself returning to the dedication of the 1949 *College Yiddish* textbook produced by the great linguist Uriel Weinreich: "*A matone di ale, vos bay zeyere kinder in moyl vet yidish lebn*" (A gift to all those in whose children's mouths Yiddish will live). In the decades that separate us from 1949, we may have lost the ability or the right to proffer such a gift, but not the wish to do so.

This book is a gift to one child—to Sara Taibl Norich—whose presence is an even greater gift than I could have imagined.

Acknowledgments

I WAS honored to have been invited by the University of Washington's Jewish Studies Program to take part in the Stroum Lecture Series, and I am grateful to Althea Stroum, Paul Burstein, and Naomi Sokoloff, my longtime friend and interlocutor, for their kindness during my stay in Seattle.

My thanks to the anonymous readers for the University of Washington Press for their comments and suggestions and to Alexandra Hoffmann, Joshua Lambert, Daniel Mintz, and Benjamin Pollak—graduate students past and present who were superb research assistants and whose passion for literature, for scholarship, for Yiddish, for American Jewish culture, (for deadlines), and for getting things right has been inspiring. I have benefited enormously from my colleagues in the Department of English and the Frankel Center for Judaic Studies at the University of Michigan. The Fellows with whom I participated in the theme year "Jewish Languages" at the Frankel Institute for Advanced Judaic Studies will remember parts of this work, their invaluable help in shaping it, and the errors they kept me from making.

WRITING IN TONGUES

CHAPTER 1

Translation Theory and Practice

THE YIDDISH DIFFERENCE

[W]hat objection can be made if a translator says to his reader: Here
I bring you the book as the man would have written it had he written
in German; and the reader responds: I am just as obliged to you as if
you had brought me the picture of a man the way he would look if his
mother had conceived him by a different father?

— Friedrich Schleiermacher

Ver vet blaybn, vos vet blaybn?
   Blaybn vet a vint,
Blaybn vet di blindkayt funem
   blindn vos farshvindt.
Blaybn vet a simen funem yam: a
   shnirl shoym,
Blaybn vet a volkndl fartshepet af a
   boym.

Ver vet blaybn, vos vet blaybn?
   Blaybn vet a traf
Bereshisdik aroystugrozn vider
   zayn bashaf.
Blaybn vet a fidlroyz likoved zikh
   aleyn,

ווער וועט בלײַבן? וואָס וועט בלײַבן? בלײַבן
   וועט אַ ווינט,
בלײַבן וועט די בלינדקייט פֿונעם בלינדן וואָס
   פֿאַרשווינדט.
בלײַבן וועט אַ סימן פֿונעם ים: אַ שנירל
   שוים,
בלײַבן וועט אַ וואָלקנדל פֿאַרטשעפּעט אויף אַ
   בוים.

ווער וועט בלײַבן, וואָס וועט בלײַבן? בלײַבן
   וועט אַ טראַף,
בראשיתדיק אַרויסצוגראָזן ווידער זײַן
   באשאַף.
בלײַבן וועט אַ פֿידלרויז לכּבוד זיך
   אַליין,

Zibn grozn fun di grozn veln zi
  farshteyn.
Mer fun ale shtern azsh fun tsofn
  biz aher,
Blaybn vet der shtern vos er falt in
  same trer.
Shtendik vet a tropn vayn oykh
  blaybn in zayn krug.
Ver vet blaybn, got vet blaybn, iz
  dir nit genug?

      Avrom Sutzkever, *Lider
      fun togbukh*, 1974[1]

זיבן גראָזן פֿון די גראָזן וועלן זי
פֿאַרשטיין.
מער פֿון אַלע שטערן אַזש פֿון צפֿון ביז
אַהער,
בלײַבן וועט דער שטערן וואָס ער פֿאַלט אין
סאַמע טרער.
שטענדיק וועט אַ טראָפּן ווײַן אויך בלײַבן אין
זײַן קרוג.
ווער וועט בלײַבן? גאָט וועט בלײַבן, איז דיר ניט
געַנוג?

אברהם סוצקעווער, לידער פֿון טאָגבוך, 1974

Who will last? And what? The wind
  will stay,
And the blind man's blindness
  when he's gone away,
And a thread of foam—a sign of
  the sea—
And a bit of cloud snarled in a tree.

Who will last? And what? A word
  as green
As Genesis, making grasses grow.

And what the prideful rose might
  mean,
Seven of those grasses know.

Of all that northflung starry stuff,

The star descended in the tear will
  last.
In its jar, a drop of wine stands fast.

Who will remain, what will remain?
  A wind will stay behind.
The blindness will remain, the blind-
  ness of the blind.
A film of foam, perhaps, a vestige
  of the sea,
A flimsy cloud, perhaps, entangled
  in a tree.

Who will remain, what will remain?
  One syllable will stay,
To sprout the grass of Genesis as on
  a new First Day.
A fiddle-rose, perhaps, for its own
  sake will stand
And seven blades of grass perhaps
  will understand.

Of all the stars from way out north
  to here,
That one star will remain that fell
  into a tear.
A drop of wine remaining in a jar,
  a drop of dew.

| Who lasts? God abides—isn't that enough?
<div align="center">Translated by Cynthia Ozick[2]</div> | Who will remain, God will remain, is that enough for you?
<div align="center">Translated by Barbara and Benjamin Harshav[3]</div> |

As the twenty-first century proceeds, Avrom Sutzkever's (1913–2010) questions are haunting. With each passing year, his queries read increasingly like a meditation on the fate of his poetic language, on the future of memory and of poetry, on the fate of the Jews. Who and what, indeed, will remain of Eastern European Jewish culture? What will remain of Yiddish?

One inescapable response is that translations will remain. Of course, even raising the issue of Yiddish texts no longer in Yiddish is treading on dangerous ground. I do not want to distract our task with the familiar, and more voluble, polemics: that Yiddish as a spoken language is in drastic decline; that it is spoken now primarily in Haredi or Hasidic (ultra-Orthodox) Jewish communities; that it has acquired a strange, almost cultic and certainly heralded status in universities; that a shockingly small number of people can read and write in the once abundant language. Jews and scholars around the world have gotten very good at arguing about all of these issues. But there can be no argument about the existence and necessity of translation. For most of the late twentieth century, and certainly in our own day, Yiddish texts have unquestionably been more familiar to more people in English translation than in their original.

That fact is not likely to change anytime soon, and it makes translation an increasingly urgent project. It also raises a number of questions we must now add to Sutzkever's pressing ones. What considerations guide translators in their choice of what to translate and how? To what extent are the old arguments about fidelity to the original or focus on the recipient still at work in the choices that translators make? Although most of Yiddish literature has never been translated, a large number of works have been translated many times. Why? This book is particularly concerned with that last question, as we follow the translation histories—what have been called (most famously by Walter Benjamin) the afterlives or second lives—of a number of well-known Yiddish texts as they have been interpreted and reinterpreted by translators in the past century. I ask what we can learn by comparing these translations, what they tell us about the history of Yiddish in America, about transformations both in Jewish American culture and in translation theory and practice. I seek, as well, to read translations back through the originals, considering the nuances of word choices, the resonance of Yiddish words lost and gained in translation, grammatical shifts, and the role of varying intertexts we may trace in Yiddish and English.

The two translations of Sutzkever's poem were published at almost exactly the same time, a time when Sutzkever himself was still the *éminence grise* of Yiddish letters, living in Tel Aviv, a vibrant answer to the question of *ver vet blaybn* (who would remain). Some of the challenges faced by translators are certainly contained in that pivotal word *blaybn*, which emerges as a refrain in the poem.

Blaybn: to remain, to stay, to be left over.

Cynthia Ozick's questions—who and what will *last*?—may seem ever so slightly more anxious than Barbara and Benjamin Harshavs' version, which asks, more neutrally, what will *remain*. Ozick expresses a more fatalistic sense of the future, underscoring the question of endurance, wondering whether or not we are witnessing the last of Yiddish. It is important to note that the Yiddish original is in the future tense, repeating the future auxiliary (וועט/*vet*) a total of fourteen times in ten of its twelve lines. Ozick's translation explicitly names the English future tense (will) only four times, in three of its lines, and the Harshavs use it twelve times in seven lines. Ozick, then, gives us a poem that is grammatically as well as hermeneutically more focused on the past than the future, less willing or able to name that future, less secure in the belief that it can be articulated.

In their final lines, too, the translators ask questions that are variations on Sutzkever's line, which can be literally translated as "What will remain, God will remain, isn't that enough for you?" The Harshavs keep the awkward punctuation but drop the negative construction; Ozick keeps the negative but neither the addressee (*you* in the familiar דו/*du* form) nor the future tense, nor Sutzkever's punctuation. Ozick's questions are more rhetorical than the Harshavs', answering the question of who remains with an assertion about the timelessness of God and a question ("isn't that enough?") that invites an affirmative answer. The Harshavs, on the other hand, reproduce Sutzkever's run-on sentence, but in erasing the rhetorical negative, they leave more open the question of whether God is a sufficient answer.

From a mere few words emerges a great span of choices and possibilities;

we suddenly see the same poem but in three quite different casts. There are other significant differences between the translations, but this close reading of this one line already reveals a central premise of this book: translation sends us back to the original, asking us not to adjudicate among variant translations or to enter into debates about the Yiddish author's intention, but rather to reread the original or to compare the translations in order to enter into the ongoing act of interpretation. Taken together, these two translations contain the tensions revealed in Sutzkever's poem. Their different emphases echo his questions about the future and the past, about mourning, about Yiddish in Israel or anywhere in the world, about God and the possibilities for re-Genesis. They remind us, as Sutzkever does in so much of his poetry, about the necessity of confronting these questions and the impossibility of definitive, timeless answers to them.

The need for translation in Western culture, and among Jews, is commonly traced to the familiar Tower of Babel story, which is to say that it is traced to the human desire to understand and interpret and the hubris implied in that desire. (One of the most influential studies of translation, published by George Steiner in 1975, is titled *After Babel*.) Jewish thought and theories of translation meet in and around the Bible, not only in the Tower of Babel or the many studies of Bible translation that are foundational for translation studies, but also in a number of verses and liturgical allusions. In her comprehensive study of translation, Naomi Seidman calls our attention to a compelling interpretation of a verse from the Book of Nehemiah. Nehemiah 8:8 ("they read in the book, in the Law of God, distinctly; and they gave the sense and caused them to understand the reading" [Jewish Publication Society (JPS) translation]) has been read as referring both to translation (into the vernacular) and to interpretive commentary, underscoring the inextricable bonds between these two enterprises.[4]

Sometime between the third and first centuries BCE (scholars differ about this dating), the Septuagint—the first translation of the Hebrew Bible into Greek—was produced, undeniable evidence of the need for and anxiety about translation. According to a familiar legend, the Septuagint was the product of seventy-two (some say seventy) scholars who were summoned from all the tribes of Israel and placed in separate rooms for seventy-two (or seventy) days. At the end of this period, each one emerged with a perfect translation, and, in keeping with the nature of perfection, all of their translations were identical, ultimate proof of the divinely inspired success of this enterprise.

Furthermore, some considered this translation (or these identical translations) superior to the original.

This is, no doubt, an exceedingly intimidating model of translation. It suggests that successful translations can only be achieved by divine intervention, surely a view of the translator that even the most inspired poets have been reluctant to claim for themselves. It suggests, further, not only that translators seek to create the one definitive translation of a text but also that such a translation must suffice for all eternity. Moreover, it challenges translators to improve on the originals before them. As if daunted into a kind of dull literalness by this vision of what translation should be, some later versions of the Bible sought exact renditions that resulted in stilted, word-for-word literal translations that ignored grammar, syntax, and even meaning in the target language.

The translation of more worldly texts must be held to more mundane standards than these. Yet in the case of modern translations of Yiddish, the expectations and the resulting disappointments seem almost as fraught. With its decline, Yiddish has become the sacred Jewish tongue, the language that must be preserved intact, the ineffable connection to a lost past—threatened by yet more losses each time it is given over to another idiom. In almost every text and commentary, Yiddish translators seem to remind themselves and their readers with startling regularity of the etymological links among translation, transgression, and aggression. Translators literally carry something over from one place (or language) to another. In doing so, they transgress by definition—they step across or beyond their point of origin. And the act of aggression—attack—thus performed is inevitable. The etymological connections are almost identical in Yiddish. The Yiddish איבערזעצונג (iberzetsung/translation)—like the German *Übersetzung* from which it derives—contains a similar notion of things being placed elsewhere, carried over, set down.[5] And it is aggressive, containing within it a verb used for hitting or striking. Hebrew has its own version of this homology. In Hebrew, to cross over (*l'avor*) is not necessarily a sin (*aveira*), but the roots are identical and so are the dangers. Hebrew, however, does not make translation (*tirgum*) a threatening act in Jewish culture.

Yiddish has several words for the act of translation, each of them derived from German. Taken together they offer a view of the wide range of translational possibilities. In addition to *iberzetsn*, we have *fartaytshn* and *dolmetchn*. A *dolmetcher* is a simultaneous translator, an interpreter (as in the English use of "interpreter for the deaf") who works primarily with oral speech; a *dolmetcher* is constrained by stricter notions of literalness and fidelity to the original.[6] *Fartaytshn* refers specifically to rendering something into the vernacular, Yiddish. Deriving from the German, or *daytsh* (the name of the language itself), it connotes "meaning" or "interpretation." Originally used for the rendition of biblical and exegetical material into the vernacular of medieval Ashkenazic Jews, the focus in *taytsh* is on making these texts comprehensible and thereby useful. A literary translation is most commonly called an *iberzetsung*, and its concern is inextricably with meaning, interpretation, and form at once. To some extent, these have become overlapping terms, but they are not interchangeable since, like the theories of translation we will encounter below, they emphasize different aspects of the translation process.

Yiddish translations of every kind often receive the kind of criticism famously attributed to Rabbi Yehuda centuries after the appearance of the Septuagint. The Talmud (B. Kiddushin, 49a) records Rabbi Yehuda's pronouncement that "one who translates a verse literally is a liar; one who adds to it is a blasphemer and a libeler." (The Yiddish nonjudgmental version might be that one who translates a verse literally is a *dolmetcher*; one who adds to it is an *iberzetser* and a *fartaytsher.*) The contemporary lament, expressed less provocatively perhaps but with no less vehemence, is that—almost inevitably—"something is lost in the translation."

Yiddish readers fear that what is lost is not only culturally specific nuances, the *tam* (taste, flavor) of the original, but the history and culture of a people. Yiddish may make contradictory but nonetheless accurate claims of being, at once, tied to a specific past that assimilation, the Holocaust, and Stalin have decimated and, also, to being a world literature, part of secular Western culture, in conversation with the European languages among which it lived. More common, among translators and their critics, is the question of how this Jewish language, steeped as it is in Jewish ritual and lore, can be understood in non-Jewish languages. Yiddish readers need no gloss for *tallis un t'fillin, Elul, Parshas Noyekh, vaser af kashe,* but English readers will need a fair amount of patience—or footnotes—to understand the resonance of "prayer shawl and phylacteries," "the Hebrew month in which the Jewish New Year is celebrated," "the week in which the Torah portion (beginning with Genesis 6:9) concerning Noah is read," and "water for a kind of porridge." This, of course, is precisely the issue with which translators are always struggling, and Yiddish should be considered no more or less difficult to translate than any other modern language. But in Yiddish these commonplace translation problems can assume epic proportions as speaking populations diminish, and we recall their turbulent histories in this century.

The lament about what is lost in translation is actually a lament about the history of the Jews in the twentieth century and about the present (and presence) and future of Yiddish. Some of the prickliness among Yiddishists is due to the inescapable necessity of translation—the increasingly frenzied sense by writers of or about Yiddish that one has no choice but to work in, think in, and translate into another language—and also to the kinds of popular and scholarly responses much of our work elicits. As a reader, speaker, teacher, and critic of Yiddish literature I am frequently asked a series of questions that I wish I could dismiss wittily, with no hint of pique. After lectures on Yiddish literature, more than a few audience members have asked, "Do you really speak Yiddish?" Also common: "Can there be a future for Yiddish?" "Do non-Jews take your classes? Why?" "What's it like to work in a dead language?" With academic audiences, the questions change, but one can hear the similar concerns underlying them: "How does one write about noncanonical texts without plot summaries or a deluge of elementary explanations of cultural context?" "What's it like to work in a language most of your readers cannot read?" "Who is your audience?" And above all else, there is always that other question that lingers: "Why? Why Yiddish? What is the point?"

Even if all of these questions were answered—indeed, could be answered—there would still be the often unuttered but always underlying questions about the history of Yiddish and its speakers: "Isn't your enterprise a kind of rescue operation, made all the more poignant or all the more urgent by (what is euphemistically referred to as) twentieth-century Jewish history?" "If Yiddish offers a view of pre-Holocaust Jewish culture, how can you be 'critical' or 'objective' or dispassionate about that culture after its horrible destruction?" "Who speaks for this culture now? And how?"

Increasingly, all of us—translators, teachers, critics, readers—speak for and of Yiddish in tongues that are foreign to it. Every teacher of Yiddish I know laments the situational plight of our students and ourselves. Even though we can send our students to various university language programs all over the world, there is no home, no Yiddishland where they can go to be immersed in the language. Similarly, many of us feel just a little silly when we set up language exercises in which we ask our students to engage in the kinds of role-playing conversational practices that are the staple of introductory courses in other languages. Unless they plan to live in a (very) few select neighborhoods in Brooklyn or Jerusalem or elsewhere—in which case they are very unlikely to be exposed to the kinds of secular literary texts that are the subject of this book—we can't seriously ask them to practice asking for bus directions in Yiddish, or ask them to learn how to do their banking in Yiddish, or order in a restaurant, or plan a social event.[7] (Let me be clear: many of us set up precisely such situations, but we do so self-consciously, with more than a touch of irony.)

Contemporary audiences are considerably more sentimental about the culture of Yiddish than even its most active practitioners were. Romanticized American notions of shtetl life and tradition—as the site of community support and unity, of simple but honest living, of faith and acts of charity—are only one expression of this sentimentalism. The familiar use of phoenix-like images—suggesting that Yiddish as a spoken language or a creative medium will once again rise—is a different but no less deluding kind of romanticization. Some of the choices translators make in the works I analyze in the following pages are yet another. Popular Yiddish culture now consists not of poetry or drama or fiction but primarily of klezmer music and, oddly, of something called "Yiddish dance." It consists, in other words, of fewer and fewer words; it is in danger of becoming completely inarticulate. Jeffrey Shandler, who has analyzed this phenomenon most fully and sympathetically, controversially refers to contemporary Yiddish as "postvernacular." Those who use (some of) its words need not know the language; they can use it electively and selectively and still "profess a profound, genuine attachment to Yiddish." No longer necessary (or in most places, possible) as a language of daily use, postvernacular Yiddish has, as Shandler explains, "shifted from a cultural means to a cultural end."[8] To put it another, no less controversial way, as Benjamin Harshav emphasizes, what we must analyze now is the "semiotics of Yiddish," its symbolic use, what it signifies beyond the meaning of its words.[9]

Perhaps the best evidence of this shift can be seen by comparing the works translated *into* Yiddish two or three generations ago and today. Yiddish readers at the beginning of the twentieth century had access to the classics of world literature in their mother tongue: the Hebrew Bible; Shakespeare; eighteenth- and nineteenth-century novels and poetry from Russia, England, Germany, and the United States; and more. Today, the possibilities for reading new translations into Yiddish consist primarily (but, to be sure, not exclusively) of children's books: *Winnie the Pooh, The Cat in the Hat, The Little Prince, The*

Very Hungry Caterpillar, Curious George, or *One Fish, Two Fish.* These have been created no doubt to help children learn Yiddish (although often printed in transliteration) but also to show that it can be done.[10]

Yiddish and the act of translation often seem to mirror each other, subject as they have both been to mystification, protectionism, and sentimentalism. Whether translating into or out of Yiddish, liberties are believed to be taken that would be unforgivable in other languages. Translators are accused of taking liberties when translating into Yiddish in order to make the text more acceptable for a Jewish audience—expunging Christian practices and beliefs, for example. Often, translators into Yiddish are accused of condescending to their readers, as if those readers cannot really understand the canon of Western culture because they do not have the same conception of, for example, love, patriotism, or war—all claims we will encounter in the following pages. Translators out of Yiddish are accused of simply not understanding the language or its Jewish specificity. In either case, the supposition is that Yiddish compels one to revise and adapt radically in order to be understood.

As the saying goes—and it will raise a smile and a knowing nod on the face of any Yiddish speaker—the literatures of the world are "*fartaytsht un farbesert*" (translated, interpreted, and improved) into Yiddish. In the act of rendering texts into *taytsh*—Yiddish—they are, as we have seen, necessarily interpreted in order to become useful, that is, presumably to teach the Yiddish reader something about the ways of the larger world. Or, in the case of contemporary translations into Yiddish, to show that Yiddish remains versatile and *au courant*, supple enough to accommodate all sorts of modern expression.

This pithy phrase has taken on the force of urban legend. At Berkeley, a 2005 academic conference on translation and Yiddish culture was titled "Fartaytsht un Farbesert." Search for these words in print or on the Internet and you will find numerous references to the "fact" that Yiddish works often carried the title of a text, the author's name, and then "*fartaytsht un farbesert fun . . .*" (translated and improved by . . .), as in "*King Lear,* translated and improved by . . ." The joke, of course, depends on the supposedly enormous gap between high culture and spoken Yiddish. How could *King Lear* or *Hamlet* or other works be understood by a Yiddish audience unless they were offered in another, "improved" version, brought down to (Yiddish) earthiness? But surely the joke depends, as well, on the perceived chutzpah of Yiddish, its supposed arrogant pride, the audacity of claiming that it can do just about anything better than it has been done before. Or, to put it another way, as the writer Peter Manseau said in a *New Yorker* interview: "It was not uncommon to see on the title page of Yiddish translations of Shakespeare or Dickens the words '*fartaytsht un farbesert*'—translated and improved—as if some anonymous Yiddish scribbler got his hands on *King Lear* and thought, I'll just punch this up a bit."[11]

A more apt response to this claim is "*nisht geshtoygn, nisht gefloygn*" (didn't rise, didn't fly).[12] In other words, it never happened. At that same Berkeley conference (and in personal communication subsequently), the historian Michael Stanislawski said that, after careful searching, he could find not a single copy of any Shakespearean adaptation into Yiddish that carried any such attribution.[13] But the fact that no one who points to this supposedly common practice of translating and improving ever marshals proof—citations, playbills, title pages of plays, manuscripts, or advertisements—has done nothing to diminish the strength of the claim.

Underlying all this posturing about Yiddish is one of the fundamental questions of translation, which can be posed in endless ways: Whom does a translation serve? To whom does it owe fealty? Is its primary concern for the reader or the writer of the original? Is it for the target language (into which the translator translates) or the source language (out of which he or she translates)?

The question of audience is fundamental to any consideration of translation. It is also the cause of much debate and obfuscation. Walter Benjamin's "The Task of the Translator" is, arguably, the founding (and most opaque) text of modern translation theory. The theorist Paul de Man (who has been charged with a similar opacity) put the 1923 essay succinctly in context when he wrote that it "is a text that is very well known, both in the sense that it is very widely circulated, and in the sense that in the profession you are nobody unless you have said something about this text."[14] And, in a statement that will not help clarify the difficulties despite its excellent analysis of the essay and the problems of translation, Carol Jacobs has convincingly suggested that "Benjamin defines translation as untranslatable."[15]

Benjamin's essay begins with a famous, arguably startling, sentence: "To know a work of art or a genre well, it is of little use to take heed of the audience, of the respondent."[16] His insistence continues to reverberate, and, as we shall see in the following chapters, we can discern its effects in translations into English published after 1968, when the English version of his essay first appeared.

In the past half century, a translation has increasingly been understood as serving the original text and not the innocent reader; the reader is made to work harder, to perceive his or her own language as strange. Translators are now more likely to foreignize the target language rather than obscure the differences between source and target.[17] Our contemporary vision of translation has also been influenced by the analyses of Itamar Evan-Zohar, who has himself followed in Benjamin's philosophical footsteps. Evan-Zohar seeks to undo the distinctions between "high" and "low" cultures, "center" and "periphery," and even "translated" and "original." This more dynamic understanding of culture and of translation has obvious implications for Yiddish and other cultures in which diglossia is the norm. Published in 1978, his "The Position of Translated Literature within the Literary Polysystem" argued for the significance of translated texts to any understanding of culture, and within any cultural system.[18] For scholars of translation such as Lawrence Venuti and Susan Bassnett, the 1970s mark a fairly clear line of demarcation in which translations became increasingly interdisciplinary, international, and both academically respectable and culturally significant.[19] (The multiple translations of a Yankev Glatshteyn poem, considered in chapter 4, will illustrate this shift in aesthetics and politics of translation more fully.)

Benjamin's essay, to which all considerations of translation inevitably return, insists that neither the original nor the translation is intended for a reader, or created with the expectation of a particular readerly response. Before going on to argue that a translation is intended for readers who do not understand the language of the original, he asserts that "no poem is intended for its reader, no painting for its viewer, no symphony for its listener."[20] Instead, he writes, the task of the translator is "to find in the translator's language that latent structure which can awake an echo of the original."[21]

But what is that "latent structure"? If an echo gives us back the sound made by the speaker—altered, repeated, as if from a distance, but nonetheless clearly identifiable as that original sound—then exactly what must the translator do to produce it? These are the open-ended questions that plague translators and theorists alike, and some of the other foundational questions that guide this book. Such questions are not unlike that other impossible-to-answer one: What makes a good work of art? Like Justice Potter Stewart's infamous definition of pornography (*Jacobellis v. Ohio*, 1964), we may not be able to define a good translation, but most readers and critics claim to know it when they see it.

The translations considered in this study, and the comparisons I am suggesting among them (and between them and the Yiddish original), suggest that, in practice, translators are deeply engaged with their audience, concerned with what that audience may understand, how they will receive and respond to the Yiddish work. In this regard, they may seem different from the post-1968 trend I have been describing in which the reader is expected to work harder to discern meaning and cultural nuances. But that is only part of the story told in the following chapters. As Benjamin reminds us, no good translation can show the marks of a concern for the reader. This tension is the tightrope on which the translators considered here precariously walk and on which they are accompanied by translators of other languages as well. They must find the "latent structure" of the original and render it comprehensible for readers who have no access to the original. The scholar's position is different and in some ways easier, with not only access to all the versions but an imperative to return to the source text as well and consider the meaning of each.

Benjamin, and certainly theorists after him, concludes that absolute faithfulness to the original must be rejected in favor of a more nuanced version allowing for more freedom from the source. The subtlety Benjamin strives for here is precisely that of a much earlier commentator. Maimonides, in a letter to his translator, Samuel Ibn Tibbon, wrote (in the twelfth century CE):

> Whoever wishes to translate and purports to render each word literally, and at the same time to adhere slavishly to the order of the word and sentences in the original, will meet with much difficulty. This is not the right method. The translator should first try to grasp the sense of the subject thoroughly, and then state the theme with perfect clarity in the other language . . . so that the subject be perfectly intelligible in the language into which he translates.[22]

In insisting on such flexibility, Maimonides seems to be looking back disapprovingly to the "slavish" translations of sacred text and forward to the analyses that Benjamin's essay would launch.

An alternative view to Benjamin's famous rejection of the reader is, of course, reader response theories, arguing as they do that the reader is an essential part of any text, effectively completing it and giving it meaning. Translation, in this view, is the ideal paradigm for reader reception theories since, as Willis Barnstone reminds us: "to translate is to read and to interpret."[23] These perspectives, which have also gained popularity in recent decades, particularly with the ascendance of postmodernist criticism, complicate any quest for fidelity to an original text, replacing it with dual loyalties: to the text and to the audience to whom it now must be made accessible.

Further, as Renato Poggioli observes—in a comment that recalls for us the contemporary situation of Yiddish—"in modern times, a national literature reveals its power of renewal and revival through the quality and number of its translators. Sometimes it is able to survive only because of their efforts."[24] Similarly, referring to writers of little-known literatures—Søren Kierkegaard, Henrik Ibsen, August Strindberg, and Nikos Kazantzakis are his examples, but surely Isaac Bashevis Singer and the other Yiddish writers considered here belong in their ranks—George Steiner reminds us that "translation into a world-language can make a general force of texts written in a local tongue." More than that, he goes on to claim, "translation can illuminate, compelling the original, as it were, into reluctant clarity. . . . It can, paradoxically, reveal the stature of a body of work which had been undervalued or ignored in its native guise."[25] Rather than the model of loss and lack suggested by those who lament the necessity of translations from Yiddish, these more optimistic perspectives assert the value of translations not only for the target language (English) but also for its source (Yiddish) and insist that translation informs and transforms both.

These are undeniably old debates, made none the clearer by an often-repeated lament, echoing Benjamin's own, that translation is simply impossible.[26] Of course, it is not only possible but necessary. We have abundant evidence of it even in Yiddish, where the (just) lament is that not enough is translated. The question governing the following chapters is not whether translation is possible but how it is done and what it does.

Those who translate from one language to another—professionally or in their daily lives, as *iberzetsers* or *dolmetchers*—occupy an odd position. It is a position that requires mediation between two poles: between what John Keats referred to as "negative capability" and what has been called by Harold Bloom "the anxiety of influence."[27] In warning against the conscious struggle after a particular effect, Keats cautioned that such a struggle blurs a sensitive and nuanced response. He reminded us, as well, that the writers we most admire have the capacity to allow other voices and perspectives to speak through their words, muting their own tones in order to allow others to be heard.[28] The translator, too, creates a text in which the tones of the original are heard clearly, even through a different language. At the same time, the translator is subject to the challenges that Bloom outlined in his study of romantic poets:

that to be a "strong poet" artists depend on their precursors, rewrite them, and, in effect, destroy them in order to supersede them. In forging a path that combines these romantic and Freudian models, translators assume the role of the artist. Sometimes, as in the story of the Septuagint, they assume an even greater role. It should be evident that such models are more suggestive as critical conceits than as practical suggestions. None of this is in any way unique to Yiddish, although, as I have been suggesting, the case of Yiddish dramatizes the burden and the power of translation and of the translator in significant ways.

In any case, those of us who study Yiddish materials know that we must translate if we are to speak to the scholarly and popular audiences among whom we live and whom we seek to address. And yet, in ways I hope to illuminate, the very act of translation from Yiddish can seem like an act of betrayal, an act of destruction directed at a culture already devastated by much more violent acts of betrayal in the twentieth century. The situation is not helped by those who hold the exact opposite view: that only by defying demographics, only by preserving this culture in any form imaginable, can the culture of Ashkenazic Jewry survive. Both views compel us inevitably to measure our work against standards that might have worried even the scholars of the Septuagint.

The cultural politics of Yiddish translation impart an urgency to the task that rarely besets most translators. Very few of us grumble about the latest Spanish novel being translated into English or the need to translate Russian or Greek classics into English. If anything, such translations are almost always seen as proof of a text's ongoing significance. But in the contradictions and tensions that have marked its development, Yiddish is not quite like most modern languages. It has had an extraordinary history of schools and political affiliations and cultural publications, extraordinary in part because, as is often noted, it has never been the language of any nation, never had boundaries or armies or universities, even when it had an impressive array of educational and publishing institutions. It has always been peripatetic, following the geographic shifts of Jewish history. Despite—and in some cases precisely because of—this lack of stability, Yiddish has been analyzed not just as a language but as a thriving culture. Particularly in the twentieth century, the corollary to this wandering is that modern Yiddish became a cosmopolitan, international, multilingual culture. Though devoid of a "national" literature like that of France or Germany, Yiddish literature and Yiddish speakers were no less unified by a sense of a shared past and present and thus no less insistent on possessing a national culture. Frantz Fanon's definition of a national culture applies equally to the culture of Yiddish: "A national culture is the whole body of efforts made by a people in the sphere of thought to describe, justify, and praise the action through which that people has created itself and keeps itself in existence."[29]

The peculiarities of Yiddish culture have, perhaps ironically, mitigated some of the problems faced by Yiddish translators. Every writer of Yiddish, and virtually every reader as well, has always been multilingual. The history of post-Enlightenment Yiddish literature reveals not a single writer whose sole language was Yiddish; most, in fact, began writing in another language (most often, Russian, Polish, or Hebrew) or, at some point in their lives, turned to another language (most often German or English, and later modern Hebrew). Before America became a Jewish center, modern Jews were, as the Yiddish linguist Max Weinreich described them, an interlinguistic community, governed by a unique triptych of languages moving among Yiddish as vernacular, Hebrew as sacred tongue, and the languages of the lands in which they lived.[30] Of necessity, then, Yiddish has always been permeable, open to other literary influences, looking to other languages and traditions, in dialogue with them. This multilingual cultural exchange may make Yiddish literature peculiarly adaptive to translation, despite popular notions of its untranslatability.

Furthermore, at least since the Holocaust and arguably much before it, Yiddish writers were already anticipating the translations of their works. Cynthia Ozick's well-known story "Envy; or, Yiddish in America" describes a writer who desperately seeks a translator so that his poetry will live. Encountering a much-touted Yiddish prose writer (reminiscent of the persona and reputation of Isaac Bashevis Singer), this poet (perhaps a veiled representation of Yankev Glatshteyn or of any number of major but forgotten Yiddish modernists in America) can only wonder at their very different cultural fates.[31] Attributing his own obscurity neither to the fact that he is a poet in an age when fiction reigns nor to the accessibility or quality of his poetry, this poet insists that he is unknown because he writes in Yiddish. A translator is his only hope for having what Benjamin described as an afterlife.

There can, in the first decades of this century, no longer be any serious debate about whether Yiddish texts should be translated, but there is considerable argument about what to translate and how. There are some things that translation cannot hope to convey. In the case of the movement from Yiddish to English, one of those things that inevitably gets lost is—in the most literal and material sense—perception. The physical and spatial relations of text on the page are different in Yiddish and English. In the most obvious ways, English readers use their eyes differently, moving from left to right instead of right to left. In addition, Yiddish contains diacritical marks that simply cannot be replicated in English. I do not want to make too much of this difference, but the possibilities contained in how and what one sees cannot be ignored either.

Consider a trenchant example, taken from the Yiddish text and three English translations of Anna Margolin's poem "Maris tfile" ("Mary's Prayer").[32] (Anna Margolin was the nom de plume of Rosa Lebensboym, who was born in Belarus in 1887 and died in New York in 1952.) Mary addresses God familiarly in the poem. Margolin's final line in the poem is "*geyst vi a breyte blitsndike shverd.*" Kathryn Hellerstein translates that line as "Pass like a broad, flashing sword." Lawrence Rosenwald translates it as "Go like a broad and glittering sword." Shirley Kumove has "You pass like a broad, flashing sword."[33] (See appendix A, where these three translations appear in full.) All agree that the implied subject of the sentence concluded by this line is "you" (Kumove, indeed, adds the "you" into the line to offer a complete sentence), and, from each translation, it is clear that the "you" refers to God. They are each certainly correct. But there is a strong misreading possible in the Yiddish that cannot be conveyed in English and that underscores the problem of translating from one alphabet to another, from one set of markings and the meanings they connote to another. The relevant symbols do not signify in English orthography, and are barely noticeable to the English-reading eye, but they contain within them the possibilities for my misreading.

Read the Yiddish גײסט /geyst as גײַסט/gayst, read ײ as ײַ—that is, change not even a letter in the Yiddish but only the diacritical markings below that indicate vowels (and that, in any case, are often missing in printed texts)—and you have another intriguing possibility. *Gayst* (spelled *giml*, two *yud*s with a *pasekh* under them—a small horizontal line under a doubling of the smallest letter of the alphabet—*samekh, tet*) may simply be the Polish-Yiddish pronunciation of the standard verb form *geyst* (*giml*, two unadorned *yud*s, *samekh, tet*). But *gayst* also means "spirit" (or "genius") and may thus imply another voice and another tone. Uttering "*gayst,*" the speaker not only addresses God familiarly but invokes the notion of her own spirit and genius as well, offering a simile between that spirit and the power and danger of a sharp, cutting weapon: "spirit, like a broad, flashing sword." It is impossible to know if Margolin wanted to strengthen her voice in this way, but it is surely relevant to our understanding of the poem. Once again, comparing translations compels us back to the original and emphasizes the urgent need for many, varied translations.

The following chapters explore that variety. Considering a select group of works that have made their way into American culture (and, at least in the case of Isaac Bashevis Singer and Sholem Aleichem's *Tevye der milkhiker* [*Tevye the Dairyman*], far beyond) through translation into English or into film, we follow a path that readers need never take: we compare versions, often many versions, of the same text in order to trace historical, ethical, and aesthetic shifts. Within the huge variety and sheer volume of writing in Yiddish in the twentieth century, a miniscule fraction—no more than 2 or 3 percent—has been translated into English. However, the texts we focus on in the following chapters—Sholem Aleichem's *Tevye*, Isaac Bashevis Singer's stories, Yankev Glatshteyn's or Kadya Molodovsky's poetry, I. L. Peretz's story "Bontshe Shvayg," and others—have been translated in abundance. These texts offer varying perspectives from which to consider the issues of translation explored throughout. In the case of the *Tevye* cycle or of Singer's story "Yentl the Yeshiva Boy," we must consider the challenges of translating Yiddish fiction not only into English but also onto stage and screen. Singer's texts also offer a productive blurring between "original" and "translated" and underscore the extent to which translation is an act not only of interpretation but also of composition and redaction, highlighting the importance of considering the cultural and material means of production. The considerations of Glatshteyn and of Molodovsky track the extent to which reception is affected by shifts in history and in literary taste and how such shifts may result in dramatically different translations.

Why do these poems and stories attract so many iterations? What has made Tevye in particular such an enduring figure—and exactly what is it that has endured? How was Peretz's story understood in his own day, and how is it understood in ours? Why do English readers and critics pay more attention to Singer than his Yiddish readers ever did? How is Glatshteyn's tone of pained, bitter defiance conveyed in a different language and context? What can Molodovsky claim on behalf of the Jews in 1945 that only later translations are willing to reassert?

One surprising and wonderful perception that emerges throughout this study is that Yiddish texts are often more radically modern and modernist, more risky, more irreverent than their English counterparts. As we will see, the Yiddish texts are less deferential to the culture they examine and to the readers who will encounter them. These Yiddish writers are not guests who want to sit at the head table; they do not feel the need to be on good behavior, to be polite, to hope for an invitation back.

The Yiddish and English versions must and can ultimately stand alone, but there is a kinship among them that cannot be ignored. The vast majority of us will read Yiddish authors only in English. And a few will be lucky enough to read them in their original voices. An even more exciting possibility is the discovery of a jumble of voices, a cacophony of ideas and interpretations, of originals and copies and innovations, of *dolmetchn* and *fartaytshn* and *iberzetsn*. When we see this multiplicity of texts side by side, we learn a great deal about each of them, about the contexts in which they were produced, perhaps even about ourselves as readers. Addressed to very different audiences at different cultural and historical moments, these texts seem to speak to one another, to enter into a conversation about Jewish history and identity, about assimilation and its discontents, about being at home and seeking a home, about what is read and how. Above all, they provide many fascinating answers to Sutzkever's incisive question: *"Vos vet blaybn?"*

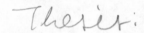

CHAPTER 2

How Tevye
Learned to Fiddle

True Wit is *Nature* to Advantage drest,
What oft was *Thought*, but ne'er so well *Exprest*.

Alexander Pope, "Essay on Criticism"

IT would be difficult to name any Yiddish work more widely known than *Fiddler on the Roof*. Except, of course, that it is not a Yiddish work at all. Still, it has made Sholem Aleichem's (1859–1916) *Tevye der milkhiker* (*Tevye the Dairyman*), or, rather, multiple versions of it, into the most transportable, international, and peripatetic Yiddish text in the modern world. No Yiddish text has been read, translated, adapted for stage and screen, analyzed, or—in some fashion—memorized more than this one. Even for those who have never read the Yiddish text or any of its numerous iterations, those who do not know that such a text exists, or those more familiar with the myth of Yiddish than with any Yiddish spoken or written word, this text has had an extraordinary afterlife. On Broadway, on-screen, in schools, repertory companies, or amateur theater troupes, communities the world over have seen and heard some version of this memorable work. It is no exaggeration to say that *Tevye* has joined the ranks of archetypal tales such as Shakespeare's *Romeo and Juliet* or *King Lear*, Mark Twain's *The Prince and the Pauper*, or Charles Dickens's *Oliver Twist*. Like those other classics, it has been frequently reincarnated or modernized, undergoing astonishing transformations through time travel and shape shifting. And all this before Harvey Fierstein ever rasped his way through the role of Tevye in *Fiddler on the Roof*, or Herschel Bernardi,

22

Chaim Topol, and Alfred Molina reprised the role first made famous by Zero Mostel, and well before Japanese and Hindi versions made their way onto YouTube.[1] In a literature that never developed the epic or had the wherewithal to crown a national poet, this story has helped Sholem Aleichem become the canonized spokesperson for Eastern European Jewish culture: part folklorist, part humorist, part historian, quintessential storyteller.

Tevye and his daughters have had an afterlife that the twentieth century denied their nonfictional compatriots. These characters have become something of a metonym for the world destroyed by the Holocaust, a destruction that Sholem Aleichem, of course, could never have imagined. To some extent, this is the fate of much of Yiddish literature that is often read backward, as if it were prophetic of the horrible times to come, as if stories of poverty or discrimination or pogroms could help us understand what came after, even as if such stories were all that Yiddish literature contained. No author has been more widely appropriated (or simply misunderstood) because of such projections (what Michael André Bernstein most resonantly called "back-shadowing") than Sholem Aleichem.[2] Whether seen as a timeless story of generational conflict, an exploration of the traditional world in the midst of modernization and revolution, an analysis of a changing economy, or love, or family, or of what is often considered the characteristically Jewish ability to laugh through tears, *Tevye the Dairyman* has been made to represent a Jewish past and present that its author would have found astonishing.[3]

The story cycle Sholem Aleichem produced between 1894–95 and 1914–16 has been widely interpreted as a collection of tales about patient, simple Jews who want only to tend their own gardens and live out their lives undisturbed, Jews who suffer because of the encroachment of modernity, the interference of anti-Semitic populations and authorities, economic and social deprivation, and more. But Tevye and other Sholem Aleichem characters can also be understood, in their own historical and social context, as rather ineffectual people facing a world they cannot comprehend, without the tools to make sense of it, without the necessary anchors of Jewish learning and faith or with those anchors rendered ineffectual by a changing world and their own inability to change.

Interpretations of Tevye himself are usually variations of two primary paradigms. He is seen as an old-fashioned *folksmentsch*, a purveyor of delightful Jewish humor, malapropisms, and misquotes of biblical and Talmudic wisdom. Or he is seen as a Job-like figure, a long-suffering Jew who argues with God but will not give up, a patriarch whose children—in Tevye's case seven daughters and in Job's case seven sons—are a series of trials he must bear. In either case, Tevye is the Jewish everyman and thus a perfect vehicle for a seemingly limitless range of interpretations.[4]

Americans are most familiar with the Tevye story through its incarnation in the musical *Fiddler on the Roof*, which traces a gradual cultural decline in the midst of a family's resilience, as embodied by the increasingly troublesome conditions of Tevye's daughters and the partners they choose and the faith and customs to which he (but not they) continues to hold.[5] But this vision, so familiar to American audiences, is not entirely Sholem Aleichem's story. All told, the Tevye tale is actually an elaborate story cycle that Sholem Aleichem developed over a twenty-year period. Tevye first appeared in 1895 in a short story in which the protagonist strikes it rich— at least by his standards—by doing a kind deed for some women who have lost their way in the woods. There was little indication here that Sholem Aleichem had a much longer work in mind. He added more Tevye stories, first publishing them as a book in 1911. It was Sholem Aleichem himself who began the reincarnation of this tale. Until his death in 1916, he continued to pen additional chapters to this work. In these additional stories, he subtracted varying numbers of daughters, changed the places to which Tevye was sent, and even altered the reasons for his departure. He would also incorporate contemporary events into the texts and even respond to his own changing financial fortunes, popularity, and, finally, wandering and illness.

קטנתי	1894	"I Am Unworthy"
דאָס גרויסע געווינס	1894	"Tevye Strikes It Rich"
אַ בוידעם	1899	"Tevye Blows a Small Fortune"
הײַנטיקע קינדער	1899	"Today's Children"
האָדל	1904	"Hodl"
חווה	1906	"Chava"
שפרינצע	1907	"Shprintse"
טבֿיה פֿאָרט קיין אֶרץ־ ישראל	1909	"Tevye Leaves for the Land of Israel"
לך־לך	1914	"Lekh-lekho" / "Get Thee Out"
וחלקלקות	1914–16	"Tevye Reads the Psalms" / "And Smoothness"

The changing tone, structure, and trajectory of the Tevye cycle is undoubtedly a reflection of the vicissitudes of its compositional history.[6] But despite the two-decade span of its creation, the text is remarkably consistent thematically.

It is worth noting that Tevye was not made into a nostalgic look back by *Fiddler on the Roof*, by Zero Mostel, Topol, or any of the actors who followed them. At its inception, the Tevye cycle was arguably already a nostalgic look back at a society that was being transformed in Sholem Aleichem's own lifetime. Several themes remain constant in the twenty years during which this text was written. One of these is the centrality of family, a theme Sholem Aleichem may be credited with inventing for Jewish literature. Another constant is Tevye's pride in his daughters' independence and intelligence. They are, as he tells all who will listen, quite capable of speaking for themselves, and they share a logic all their own. Like Tevye himself, most of them love to argue, at least one of them values books and learning, although there is no sign that she (Chava) has a great deal of either. Nor, for that matter, does Tevye himself, who can recite psalms and quote or misquote from the Bible.[7] In each story, Tevye agrees with his daughters that romance is a better basis for marriage than economics is. Through it all, his adherence to religious teachings and practices—and his conversations with God—also continues unchanged. Sholem Aleichem's characteristic outrage at the injustices of his life and times is as constant in this work as is Tevye's willingness to accommodate to a changing world in which no dogma or received wisdom can remain intact.

The stories, as he wrote them, begin with Tevye doing a good deed and being rewarded with a modest sum of money that he regards as a small fortune. He soon squanders this fortune by entering into a bad business deal with that other familiar Sholem Aleichem character, the *shlimazl* (ne'er-do-well), Menakhem-Mendl. The next five chapters are devoted to Tevye's daughters and to the inescapable dissolution of central, patriarchal authority told in their tales. We have Tsaytl, who insists on marrying for love but remains within the bounds of the family and Jewish tradition in other respects. Next we have Hodl, who also marries for love, but this time to a revolutionary whose fealty is to Marx and politics. Hodl will join her husband in his Siberian exile. Then there is Chava, whose marriage to a non-Jew is often understood as the major crisis of the work. Then Shprintse follows, the daughter who commits suicide because of unrequited love and because, the text hints, she is pregnant. She is thus the only one whose fate can never be changed.[8] And finally there is Beylke, the only one who marries for money and, in doing so, makes a terribly wrong choice and ends up in a New York City sweatshop.

Sholem Aleichem adapted the Tevye cycle just before his death when he wrote a script for both the Yiddish stage and the silent screen. He did not live to see it performed. It was revised by his son-in-law, Y. D. Berkovitch, and performed in 1919, the same year in which a silent movie was made of the stories. These productions followed Sholem Aleichem's own stage script, which made scant reference to Tsaytl and none at all to the other daughters, focusing instead on Chava's departure and return.

Toward the end of his life, Sholem Aleichem became more ambivalent about the fate of Chava than he had been during the years in which he first presented her. He kept changing his mind about what to do with her, finally invoking patriarchal tradition and Judaism itself in his deliberations. In 1905, when Chava first appeared, her marriage to a Christian had banished her from her father's embrace but not from his thoughts. In a revealing passage written in the final year of Sholem Aleichem's life, Tevye explicitly asks his interlocutor, Sholem Aleichem, and through him the reader as well, about what to do with this beloved child: "*Vos hot Tevye badarft ton?... Vi azoy volt IR zikh noyeg geven?*" (What should Tevye have done? . . . How would YOU have behaved?).[9] Readers and viewers, no doubt, are meant to understand this father's struggle sympathetically and understand why the father finally embraces his wayward child.

In the Yiddish text, Sholem Aleichem is also unable or unwilling to decide where to send his characters in the end. They cannot stay in the Ukrainian village from which they are being evicted. Russia as a whole is pogrom-ridden. America, where Sholem Aleichem himself ended up and which he had visited—quite unhappily, from 1906 to 1908—is not the promised land for Tevye, as is obvious in several of the chapters. Palestine, to which his rich boor of a son-in-law would like to exile him, may be the land promised to the Jews, but it is not at all obvious what promise it really holds. They are going to a city, but whether that city is Jerusalem, the imaginary Yehupets, Odessa, Warsaw, or New York is not apparent. Clarity will only come, says Tevye, if the messiah comes to take them elsewhere first. The ambiguity of these variant endings is undone by each of the adaptations of Tevye, whose teleological endings are more affirmative than that of the author's.[10]

It has become rather commonplace to lament the changes wrought upon Sholem Aleichem's text by time and translation.[11] But it is worth recalling that some of those changes were already anticipated by the author himself. Over the twenty-year creation of this story, the changes in Russia and the fate of its Jews are more pronounced than any character changes in Tevye himself. After the first failed Russian revolution in 1905, after the rise of the nationalist, anti-Semitic Black Hundreds, after the economic upheavals of the Russo-Japanese War, after the Beilis blood libel trial to which Sholem Aleichem refers at the end of his text, as the Dreyfus affair unfolds, and, finally, after the start of the First World War (to which he does not refer), Tevye and his creator seem to have become, understandably, more than a little weary. "My Golde was the cleverest of us all," Tevye says near the end of the book, referring to his dead wife, because "she looked around in time, said goodbye to this foolish world, and went to the next one" (149). The imagined terminus for Tevye and his daughters, then, includes forced exile to Siberia, coerced departure to Palestine or America, poverty, anti-Semitic threats, or death. For a book full of comedic resilience, this is an unlikely set of endings, but quite an understandable one given its time and place.

It is this very open-endedness that has made Tevye peculiarly adaptable to languages, media, and cultures Sholem Aleichem never encountered or imagined. It has become a text onto which various teleological, didactic, or nationalist myths can be written. In addition to the important Yiddish and English stage adaptations and the English translations of *Tevye*, there are several film versions of the story that illustrate Tevye's extraordinary adaptability. In particular, the Yiddish, English, Hebrew, and Russian films offer very different depictions of and resolutions to the plight of Tevye and his daughters. Like Sholem Aleichem, they also offer different numbers of daughters: the Yiddish film has two, the English five, the Hebrew seven, and the Russian only one. In the transition from Yiddish into other languages and, especially, in the transition from the written to the visual, each version is less a product of Sholem Aleichem's imagination and more a product of its time and place of production:

Tevye (1939)
Directed by Maurice Schwartz (Yiddish)

Tevye and His Seven Daughters (1968)
Directed by Menahem Golan (Hebrew)

Fiddler on the Roof (1971)
Directed by Norman Jewison (English)

Get Thee Out (1991)
Directed by Dimitri Astrakhan (Russian)

The first film, *Tevye*, was made in Yiddish and starred Maurice Schwartz, one of the most famous actors in the history of the Yiddish stage and screen. (He also played Tevye onstage.) It was filmed on Long Island in the summer of 1939.[12] Several of its actors came from Poland to make the film, and some of them were unable to return home following the Nazi invasion of Poland on September 1. This film is thus already a testimonial to those left behind. The film *Fiddler on the Roof* appeared in 1971, seven years after the smash Broadway musical upon which it is based. It was filmed in Croatia (Yugoslavia) and produced by Norman Jewison (whose next film would be *Jesus Christ, Superstar*) with Joseph Stein's screenplay and Jerome Bock's music.[13] The Hebrew film, *Tevye and His Seven Daughters* (written, produced, and directed by Menachem Golan), predates the English one but antedates the Broadway hit with which it seems to be in conversation.[14] Here we find not one but many fiddlers on the roof.[15] (The film had French and English subtitles, but as the Israeli viewing audience changed so did the subtitles; now Russian obscures the earlier languages.) The Russian film is titled *Izydi*, translated as *Get Thee Out*, echoing Sholem Aleichem's chapter "Lekh-lekho." It was the first film written and directed by Dimitri Astrakhan, who was to become one of Russia's most prominent filmmakers (and who, not coincidentally, as some critics point out, had a Jewish parent).[16] It appeared in 1991, in the wake of *glasnost* (openness) and *perestroika* (restructuring; the program of economic, political, and social reforms of the mid-1980s), as the Iron Curtain was falling and Russia was reimagining itself and trying to make sense yet again of its ethnic diversity and tensions. *Get Thee Out* may be the most faithful visual representation of Tevye's physical world. Filmed in Chernivtsi, Podolia (Ukraine), which had a large Jewish community until the Second World War, it reproduces the landscape and architecture of the world Tevye inhabits; (almost) entirely in Russian, it does not reproduce the Yiddish, Hebrew, or Ukrainian of that world. And in clearly depicting people who are Russians (rather than Ukrainians), it also clearly addresses the language and concerns of the Russian people in the tempestuous period leading up to the fall of the Soviet Union rather than those of the Jews of that earlier (1905) Russian revolution.[17] In other respects, too, Sholem Aleichem's stories are more inspiration than source in this film, which, the end credits tell viewers, is based on works by Sholem Aleichem, Isaac Babel, and Aleksandr Kuprin.[18] The combination of Babel and Sholem Aleichem gestures toward the two most powerful Jewish figures in the Russian cultural imagination, but there is a difficult, uneasy balance in the film between the former's view of characters and situations that often seem bestial and the latter's genial, if at times, ironic or critical view of the Jews and their surroundings.

A look at the opening scenes of each of the films, in the order of their conceptualization, is especially illuminating. In the Yiddish film, the camera transforms Tevye's monologue into a nostalgic long view of the Old Country (except that we are on Long Island) where even the non-Jewish peasants speak Yiddish—albeit a ridiculously accented Yiddish. In fact, their speech is difficult to understand in any language since, even in Russian, their mocked Ukrainian accents make them sound as if they are juggling marbles in their mouths, surely an indication of the contempt we are to feel for them and the stupidity and cruelty of which they are capable. In the love affair that is highlighted at the beginning of the film, signs of a new order of things appear in the midst of a pastoral scene. Also heralding this new order is the invocation of Maxim Gorky (who also appears in Sholem Aleichem's text). Gorky (1868–1936) was held by Sholem Aleichem and others in high estimation. A man of humble origins who had great faith in culture, opposed both the czarist regime and the violent excesses of the 1905 revolution and the anti-Semitic excesses of both, and is often associated with the precepts of socialist realism, Gorky was widely regarded as the Jews' best friend among Russian writers.

The English film resolves the conundrum suggested by this chapter's title. As Norman Jewison points out, Tevye learned to fiddle from Marc Chagall.[19] The film begins with sunrise over the shtetl, with many roofs and a fiddler atop one. All of the film was shot through a silk stocking, diffusing light and evoking a softer, less shadowy environment.[20] (In the second half, as conditions worsen, the film shows less and less color, as if to make starker—more black and white—the responses we cannot avoid having.) As the film breaks into the song "Tradition," we see ritual objects that have nothing to do with the ensuing story but that are designed to remind an audience of what it once knew or, more pointedly, to show an audience unfamiliar with their use how these Jews once lived. These declarations about continuity seem to protest a bit too much and even to hint at their own undoing. Tradition runs deep, and as Tevye tells us, because of traditions, "every one of us knows who he is and what God expects him to do." In the last thirty years of the twentieth century, one might have envied Tevye this clarity about his Jewish identity. Tradition teaches him and his community how to eat, sleep, work, and wear clothes. But, ironically, Tevye also tells the viewer that he has no idea how these traditions came to be, and as all-encompassing as the ones he points to may seem, it is worth noting that they do not include prayer, study, or religious rituals. Reinforcing traditional gender roles (Papa studies, Mama runs the house, boys go to cheder, girls learn to cook and sew), tradition here implies the opposite of the changes we are about to see in this film and the changes the audience has already seen in its own lifetime.

The items shown in this opening of the film are too rich for the humble rural homes in which they are presumably to be found. Also anachronistic is the voice of the Israeli actor, Topol, whose Israeli-British speech bears no trace of a Yiddish accent.[21] The small, isolated village (*dorf*) where Tevye lived alone as a Jew in Sholem Aleichem's story is transformed into a sizable shtetl, where he is surrounded by a large community of Jews. Nonetheless, *Fiddler on the Roof* is the intertext for all subsequent films (although the Hebrew one is most aware of the Yiddish text and film).

The Hebrew film announces a similar look back even though it is pointing toward a different destination. It begins with a song, to which the movie returns at the end. "Where is this path leading? / Where am I going? / . . . / I am going to my shtetl."[22] At the same time, there is a scrolling text in which we learn that "in the beginning of the twentieth century in Russia, about three million Jews lived in conditions of oppression and persecution. They hungered daily and suffered pogroms seasonally. In the small Ukrainian town of Anatevke lived Tevye, with his wife and his seven daughters. A lone Jew among goyim [non-Jews]. Tevye, a woodcutter, was a poor man, until one day something magical happened to him and he won a milking cow and thirty-seven rubles."[23] Only the last sentence bears any resemblance to Sholem Aleichem's story. The historical and cultural explanations are (as in each film) a product of a different context. The film does not encourage us to ask just how much value to place on those thirty-seven rubles. In 1900, this would have been worth about nineteen dollars.[24] This is not an insignificant sum for a man of Tevye's station, but it would not have been sufficient to support a family of nine for long.

In his story, Sholem Aleichem gives his readers a more complex and accurate sense of the value of this sum and thus qualifies for the reader Tevye's excitement over his windfall. Here he is also given a milking cow worth even more than thirty-seven rubles, and he is now able to improve his position significantly by setting up a business in dairy products. In the recent past, Tevye was earning two gulden (half a ruble) a day—although not, as he says, every day—carrying timber to the railroad station (9). He has, then, received about three months' wages. In 1899, when the second chapter of the story cycle was published, we learn that a cow Tevye had bought at a great bargain cost him fifty rubles; he laments the sudden death of both the cow and a calf that was worth over twenty rubles (43). In the text, Tevye evidently has a rather elastic and certainly a limited understanding of the value of money. In this, as nearly every critic of the Tevye cycle is at some pains to point out, he is not so different from the author himself, who inherited a small fortune from his father-in-law and squandered it in market speculations.[25]

Tevye twice refers to sums of money that change dramatically at the instant they are mentioned. He says, for example, that he met a rich man who was worth at least a hundred thousand rubles and maybe even millions more (16). He describes a man who had been a ne'er-do-well and was now making the extraordinary sum of twenty rubles a week, or perhaps forty (16). The omission of such details in each of the films saves Tevye from the ironic view of him that Sholem Aleichem presents. In the book, he is a man who acquires a sum of money whose value he cannot properly assess; in this film, he acquires a fortune that might well change his economic status if only he were left in peace and not subject to the anti-Semitism that surrounds him. Any consideration of value is replaced instead by a view of the family's surroundings, which, as we have already begun to see, vary considerably, with the Israeli camera emphasizing the poverty of these Eastern European Jews and the American one displaying the riches of their culture.

The Russian film opens with a dramatic, if somewhat confusing, proleptic scene. The pogrom that is shown in gory detail is both a foreshadowing of the film's ending and a backshadowing into Russian-Jewish history and continuing, disastrous relationships.[26] The viewer's perspective also shifts confusedly from present to past and future. As other similar scenes are shown, we come to realize that the film is progressing toward this inevitable end, but it is doing so in reverse, showing the ultimate scene of destruction first and ending with the first signs of the horror that is to come. It also becomes apparent that some of these scenes show what has actually taken place, while others are imagined by the main character, who fears what may become of his family. Whether fantasy or actuality, they are rendered in black and white, a stark contrast to the color that marks the present. The Russian film seems determined to undo the relationships that have led to this pogrom and expulsion, to show Russian peasants as decent, earthy men, to show that Jews are no different from them, and to underscore the repulsiveness of anti-Semitism and anti-Semites. In one of the few uses of Hebrew or Yiddish in the film, the music we hear as the pogrom unfolds is El Malei Rakhamim (God of Mercy), the liturgical Hebrew song of mourning that will be heard again and is the first of many refrains the film employs.

The film cuts away from the pogrom scene to a very different view of the here and now in which the Jew stands before a government official (in color, in an office that reflects czarist, prerevolutionary decadence) in order to obtain permission to run a dairy business. His name is not Tevye but rather Motl Salomnovitch Rabinovitch; in other words, Motl, son of Shalom Rabinowitz, the name of the author we know more commonly as Sholem Aleichem.[27] In celebration of his success, Motl does two noteworthy things. Before going home and having sex with his wife ("making love" is too delicate a term for what the film shows us, even without showing us the sex act itself), he visits a brothel, where he is well known and quite at home. And when he buys a cow, he has a large sign made announcing that "Motl and Sons" is now open for business; like Tevye, he has no sons, but that, as Tevye also knows, is not how one advertises or builds a dynasty. The sign shows two bare-breasted women, whose heavy breasts are, no doubt, meant to invoke the heaviness of the udders he has just acquired and the healthy milk they will give. The sign and the udders become another of the refrains we encounter. Russians and Jews are distinguishable from each other here only in their dress and in the exterior of their homes (the color of the door, which is blue for non-Jews, or the design of their roofs, which is shingled for Jews).[28] That is, they are distinguishable only by externals that can be put on or taken off. When he is fully clothed and outdoors, Motl looks like a traditional Jew and like no one else in the film. Clothed or naked, these are all earthy and rather unattractive figures; they are equally sensual, equally coarse, equally drunken. But they are also equally Russians, loving their families, taking care of one another, and resisting the authorities or the bigots who would destroy their communities.

The second set of scenes to be considered here depicts, in strikingly different ways, the events following Chava's marriage to a non-Jew, Fyedka. This scene in the Yiddish version may likely be the most well-known moment in all of Yiddish film. In it, as in Sholem Aleichem's text, the family mourns by sitting shiva for the departed daughter. (Although Jewish law does not require or even encourage the practice, some Jews observe the mourning ritual for a convert.) But here director Maurice Schwartz adds another ritual, first performing the Havdalah service that ends the Sabbath and divides it from the workaday week. In 1939, this was already a nostalgic gesture showing his

American and Yiddish-speaking audience a ritual they would have recognized but that they were unlikely to still be practicing. Tevye's ambivalence about rejecting his wayward daughter is nowhere clearer than in his subsequent announcement that shiva will last for no more than one hour. (In a traditional house of mourning, the family may indeed sit for only one hour following the Sabbath, but the full period of mourning resumes the next day.) Mingling rituals and observing mourning but truncating it, the Yiddish film confronts the growing concern with assimilation and intermarriage in a long, sympathetic view of the suffering family.

The American perspective, by 1971, is quite different. *Fiddler on the Roof* has no scene of shiva, no ritual mourning. Tevye is torn between his love for his daughter and his God, and, as in Sholem Aleichem's text, he chooses God. That may be his choice, but it is not the film's. Tevye literally turns his back on Chava at the end, but the camera does not. The scene ends with a focus on Chava and compels us to sympathize with her. We see not the parents sitting on the floor but the young woman left alone, bowed in sorrow, in despair.

The Hebrew film announces unequivocally that "Chava is dead," and the family members weep, remove their shoes, sit on the floor, and rend their garments (the last act is absent from the Yiddish film) to observe the seven days of mourning. En route to her church wedding, a hesitant Chava stops at her family's home and calls out to her father, who will not answer. As the wedding procession continues, it is Tevye and not Chava to whom our attention and sympathies are drawn. As if in answer to the English film's focus on a grieving Chava, the Hebrew film shows us the mourning family instead, with the inconsolable father at the center. There is no ambiguity about Chava's transgression or Tevye's reaction. The Israeli camera in 1968, months after the Six-Day War, rejects the possibility of sympathizing with those who leave, favoring the needs of the collective over those of the individual. This perspective is entirely distinct from that of the English film.

In the Russian film (where the character of Chava is called Beylke), we see initial reluctance on the part of both Christian and Jewish parents to accept this union, and we are quickly given to understand that both are wrong in their rejection of the other. Finally, in this scene, there is acceptance, first on the part of the Russian father and then by Motl as well. The only Yiddish in the movie is Motl's "mazel tov" in honor of the marriage and the reconciliation it symbolizes, followed by a rousing drinking song. "Let's all drink a glass of wine," the Jews sing in Yiddish, presumably as an indication that, although, on occasion, they may use a different language, these Jews celebrate just like other Russians. There is equality between Jew and non-Jew as they put aside parochial prejudices and accept the brotherhood of all Russians, now united by marriage and drink.

In yet another set of comparable scenes, we are shown the events precipitating Tevye's forced departure from his home. In the written text, Sholem Aleichem never described a pogrom scene, either referring to such inescapable events obliquely or avoiding them entirely. Only the Yiddish film follows him in this restraint. For later, post-Holocaust audiences, the pogrom scene, however figured, becomes an iconic part of the story of expulsion.

The Yiddish film introduces us to drunken louts, who were, in earlier scenes, merely comic. Now the threat they pose and the evil they do cannot be contained by humor, despite their obviously ridiculous behavior and speech. Tevye is treated unfairly, as are all the Jews of the Russian Empire. He must sell his belongings and leave within twenty-four hours, but there is no scene of riot and death.

In the American film, the government is directly responsible for the pogrom. Soldiers interrupt Tsaytl's wedding and wreak havoc, until their commander announces that they have done enough damage and can cease. In this scene, Tevye is certainly not isolated from other Jews; he is surrounded by hundreds of Jews in a community that celebrates and suffers together. The military commander, showing contrition, explains his actions to Tevye. "Orders are orders," he says, in words that would have been nearly universally understood as an echo of the language of the Nuremberg trials. Anti-Semitism, real enough in the time and place depicted in the film, is consistently represented in terms that evoke the Holocaust. *Fiddler on the Roof* may thus be understood as both a product of and a significant contributor to the increasing Jewish and American focus on the Holocaust that was emerging in the late 1960s and early 1970s.

In the Hebrew film, the pogrom immediately follows Chava's wedding, hinting at a causal relationship that it cannot claim and linking intermarriage with the disaster that ensues. (There is no visual or thematic linking of the two in the American film, where the pogrom scene precedes the Chava story.) Tevye's attempt to mitigate the horrors of the pogrom with humor and clever negotiation reveals the stupidity and the menace of the people who confront him. Urging his family to go into the house, Tevye addresses his peasant neighbors, reminding them that the time of pogroms has already passed elsewhere and asking why they would start one now. One peasant's answer is a version of "orders are orders." He asks Tevye what they should do and proposes various things to destroy, concluding that some sort of unpleasantness must happen. The exchange between them is humorous, until it ends in mayhem.

Tevye: If you've been ordered to, then you must make a pogrom or else the commander can make trouble for you. But maybe there is someone above that commander? And someone above that one? Above all of us there is God who sees all—your God and ours. And maybe he wants just the opposite. Who knows what God wants? Is there one among you who knows what God wants?

Peasant: We've got nothing against you. It's true that you're a Jew, but you're a good guy. Still, one thing has nothing to do with the other. We have to make a pogrom, says the commandant. Maybe you'll let us break all your windows and be done with it.

Tevye: All right, but break one window.

Peasant: Five.

Tevye: But I have only four.

Peasant: OK, then we'll break two of them.

Tevye gets the family out of the house, assuring them that their "neighbors" will only break windows. And then there is utter chaos as they smash the house and steal its belongings. This mob cannot be contained once it gets a taste of destruction. The town priest watches, unable or unwilling to do anything but help Tevye up after the mob has literally walked all over him. The exchange between Tevye and the peasant is an almost verbatim translation of an exchange near the end of Sholem Aleichem's book, with one important difference: in both, Tevye reports that the town council agreed to break windows, but the Yiddish work stops short of the turmoil that the Hebrew film shows vividly. The Israeli lesson could not be clearer or less subtle: What can the Jews expect from their surroundings? How can they take their neighbors' word for anything? How can such lawlessness be held in check?

In many ways, the Russian film contains the most complex and problematic of these scenes. On the film's set, the town stages a *fake* pogrom, forced upon good Russians by a corrupt government and perpetrated only for official eyes. Instead of destroying his home, Motl's friends set fire to the privy and put on a good show, with the Jews choosing what to break. If left alone, without outside agitators, this film is telling us, they would all get along and the true soul of the Russian people would prevail. The Russian official who appears on this scene is concerned with the appearance of lawlessness. Knowing that this is not a real pogrom, he nonetheless wishes to assert control over the situation. His solution is that he will report that there was a pogrom against Jews (which, in context, is only to be expected) but that the authorities stepped in to stop civil unrest before it got out of hand. Everything is performative, perhaps reminding viewers of the staged nature of film, but more profoundly reminding them of how Russian authorities—whether under the ousted czars or the about-to-be-ousted Communists—also performed just governance through the appearance of things that were untrue.

The endings of each of the films are equally diverse, reminding us of the different imagined viewers for whom they were intended. In the Yiddish film, as in Sholem Aleichem's text, Chava returns to a home now bereft of its matriarch and headed by a much-weakened patriarch. She must leave her husband, because, as Chava says, she has come to recognize that they are of "two different worlds." Quoting the Book of Ruth to her father (in typical fashion, Tevye mistakes the source of his daughter's words, attributing them to Ecclesiastes), Chava affirms the unity of the Jewish people even as the film reminds us of the complexity of the contemporary situation. Ruth, of course, is a convert to Judaism, not away from it, and her commitment to her mother-in-law, Naomi, and her newly adopted people results in a union that produces the Davidic line from which the messiah will come. In the intimate second-person singular form and in the future tense, Ruth says to Naomi, "Where you go, I will go; where you lodge, I will lodge; your people shall be my people, and your God my God; where you die, I will die."[29] Rather than portend a most propitious future, Chava's words are a reminder of the past and of an inauspicious fate. She addresses her father, and through him the entire Jewish people, in the polite or plural form and in the present, saying, "Where you go, I go; we share one fate." The story "Lekh-lekho" (Get thee out), upon which this scene is based, also makes clear the enormous gap between Ruth's words and Chava's. Both women embrace the Jewish people, but in doing so the latter is embracing a dreadful exilic fate. In the text, Tsaytl quotes Chava's words to their father. She said, reports Tsaytl, that "where we go, she goes; our exile is her exile" (162). In 1914, the threat of exile is very real. In the 1939 film, as the war in Europe begins and the rise in anti-Semitism in Germany and Poland has led to fears about the fate of European Jewry, Chava's invocation of *goles* (exile) has been transformed into an assertion about *goyrl* (fate).

When, at the end of Sholem Aleichem's text, Tevye asks, "What would you have done?" the only answer the text allows is the one given by Tevye himself when he asserts that a man cannot harden his heart against his children (163). In the Yiddish film, as he embraces his daughter, Tevye asks a different question of a different audience. "God, what do you say?" he asks, addressing an interlocutor who, unlike Sholem Aleichem or the reader, will neither answer nor disseminate Tevye's story. In lieu of a response, Tevye embraces his daughter at the end in an unmistakable gesture of forgiveness and unity. He tethers a goat to the back of the wagon, packs up his possessions, loads his two daughters and two grandchildren, and sets out.

Although the English film also ends with forced exile, *Fiddler on the Roof* depicts a dramatically different, infinitely more optimistic scene of departure that points forward to a better (American) future, while reminding us of the fate of those who did not leave. Golde is very much alive at the end of the film and joins her husband and younger daughters who will go to America. Tsaytl and Motl will go to the city in hopes of earning enough money to join them. (In 1971, an American audience must be terribly aware of the fate that awaits them if they are unable to emigrate.) Fyedka and Chava are leaving for Cracow, because, as he says, "some are driven away by edicts, others by silence. We cannot stay among people who can do such things to others." Once again, the film filters this turn-of-the-century story through the overpowering language of the Holocaust. Chava does not leave her husband to return to her people, but Tevye—and an American audience—do not expect her to. Instead, Tevye urges Tsaytl to say "God be with you" to the departing couple, a clear sign of acceptance and reconciliation.

As the town is emptied of its Jews, the camera focuses a sympathetic gaze on the constable who has merely been following orders. ("We wanted to show that there were people who were unable to stop everything, and . . . ," says Jewison in the commentary accompanying the DVD version of the film, unable to finish that sentence.)[30] And then we see masses of people on the move, on foot or in carts, carrying their Torah and their belongings into an uncertain future. All of Eastern European Jewry seems to be on a forced march at the film's end. It is at once a scene of *shlepping golus* (or "dragging the exile"—a Yiddish idiom meant to convey the long Jewish exilic condition), of the Exodus from Egypt, of mass migration to America, and also, and perhaps primarily, a scene invoking the Holocaust. Unable to sustain their communities, massed together by forces over which they can have no control, going off in different directions, we witness these Jews forming long lines of movement that make them part of the long line of Jewish exile. But those heading toward America have a much brighter future, into which the fiddler and "Tradition" follows them.[31] Jewison said that "the film is about the breaking down of traditions in a family."[32] Perhaps. But it is also about the myth of continuity and the promise kept by America.

It comes as no surprise that in the Hebrew film Tevye is en route to another promised land. The peasant to whom he has been forced to sell his possessions bids farewell by wishing him luck and announcing that they were "quite good neighbors." In an extraordinarily ironic line, he adds: "I hope your neighbors in Jerusalem will be no worse than we were." An Israeli audience hearing this line in 1968 would have had no trouble equating these neighbors with their own or putting equal trust in both.

At the film's end, Fyedka pursues Chava, who is running after her father's wagon. He is stopped by the priest, who urges him to let Chava go because "that is her destiny." Golde helps her daughter onto the departing wagon that Tevye has finally brought to a halt; all join in laughter, and the wagon—as in the Yiddish film, followed by a tethered goat—proceeds. To complete the unmistakable message of the film, it ends with the same song with which it began, now resonating differently. Asking where the path is leading, the song's words point to the shtetl. But that is precisely where, we know, the cart is not leading. It is moving far away from the shtetl (described here as possessing "a deserted house / . . . snow and hunger"), going in the direction of prayer, toward those other towns and villages yet to be built in the land of Israel.

The Russian film arrives at the point depicted in the beginning: the pogrom that is about to start. This combination of socialist realism, positivism, and anti-Soviet sentiment projected back onto the czarist days includes, again, liturgical mourning. In the familiar tradition of Sholem Aleichem's esteemed Gorky, this scene offers a stark look at the evil that must be undone and the new order that must come. The Jews are being attacked by outside agitators, emboldened by outside officials and policies. This is a condemnation of the way of the czars and of the Soviet regime that followed it and that, in 1991, was coming to an end. It condemns the excesses of Russian nationalist fervor, invoking the Black Hundreds of Sholem Aleichem's day and Pamyat (the People's National-patriotic Orthodox Christian movement, whose name means "memory" in Russian) of Astrakhan's.[33] This scene and, indeed the film as a whole, could not have been produced at the height of Soviet power. The new Russian order, the film tells us, must reject this anti-Semitism and the nationalistic excesses that have led to it and must be based, instead, on what we see at the end: Motl's neighbors help him flee from the advancing mob, but when he turns back to fight his enemies, his neighbors come to his aid. Once again, we hear the sounds of El Malei Rakhamim and see poor, wounded Jews leaving their homes. The approaching mob is difficult to see, emerging from the brightest, most blinding light of this film. It is impossible to discern individual faces through this glare, intensifying the terror that all must feel at the approach of this mob. The music changes from El Malei Rakhamim to a military waltz that serves as a fugue in the film, sounding at different pivotal moments, yielding to a contrapuntal crescendo that accompanies the determined, tragic defiance of Motl and the villagers who come to his aid. Sound and sight reinforce the overwhelming horror of the scene of carnage that we have already seen in earlier parts of the film. First, the camera freezes on a still shot of Motl's face; then the music stops altogether; and, finally, the advancing, blinding light encases Motl, obliterating him.

It is not surprising that each of these films changes Sholem Aleichem's text. They are strong translations from turn-of-the-century Eastern European Yiddish to dramatically different contexts and languages and, just as dramatically, from the written to the visual and audible. Each of the films offers a different solution to the problematics of rendering Tevye's monologues, addressed to Sholem Aleichem and through him to the Yiddish-reading world. In the text, his Yiddish is famously augmented with Hebrew quotations, adaptations, interpretations. In the Hebrew and Russian films, Yiddish assumes a similar role, serving as an interjection that reminds us of its characters' origins. In the Russian film, Hebrew is liturgical and Yiddish is encountered only in a drinking song. In the Hebrew film, Yiddish interjections are comic, nostalgic, and quite rare. At a wedding, for example, we hear the traditional Yiddish song "Khosn, kale, mazel tov" (Congratulations to the bride and groom). Elsewhere Tevye utters the sarcastic Yiddish exclamation "A glik hot mikh getrofn" (What a joy has befallen me) when he hears of Hodl's new love; when he hears about Gorky, this becomes the even more sarcastic "A Gorky hot mikh getrofn" (What a Gorky has befallen me). In the Yiddish film, this polyglot milieu is ridiculed in the accented Yiddish, Ukrainian, and Russian speech of the non-Jews, though the threat they pose is anything but comic. The American film is monolingual except for a mumbled (also rare) prayer and the ubiquitous and presumably familiar exclamation of "mazel tov" that accompanies the announcement of every marriage.

Tevye's long first-person monologues, directed in the stories to Sholem Aleichem himself, are transformed into something else in each of these films. Instead of monologue, we have scenery, music, and actual places and people. No viewer is under the illusion that he or she is seeing the real thing. Every viewer must contend with the knowledge of the century's history that has made it impossible to film in situ. But this was, as I have suggested, partly true for Sholem Aleichem himself, who was writing at the turn of the century and who sought to capture a type of character just as such a character was disappearing from historical view.

Readers and viewers have sought in Tevye what Sholem Aleichem himself may have sought: foundational values, ethics, coping mechanisms, and, perhaps for both writer and filmmakers, images and themes that might explain something about the Jews while also having universal implications. One of the most striking observations about the Tevye cycle and its adaptations is what they share, which is, ultimately, a focus on the family as the unit of meaning and a focus on the present of each film's creation. Tevye has been understood as a representative of the Jews, standing in for the collective. He has also been understood as an individual, caught in a struggle that is no less psychological than it is social and historical. But Sholem Aleichem's text shifts our focus away from both the collective writ large and the individual; these foundations of Judaism are actually replaced by the family as the center of gravity and significance. In the cursed year of 1941, the Soviet-Yiddish critic Meyer Weiner wrote that Tevye's "withdrawal to the family as the sole source of consolation" was one of the "historic consequences of persecutions and oppression."[34] This is precisely what Sholem Aleichem had perceived all along. The focus on the family represents something of a retreat, but an unavoidable one. It protects Sholem Aleichem (and his readers) from the despair that comes with confronting the reality of the rapidly worsening history of the Jews as the twentieth century proceeds. This is a reality that Sholem Aleichem cannot hope to change, and so he resorts to the only conceivable alternative—a narrative where these devastations are in the margins, as it were, but where the vibrant, loving family holds the center.

The film adaptations all seem to share this desire, even when they distort the text's focus on this family as isolated by placing it within a large community of other Jews (as does the English version and, in a different way, the Hebrew) or supportive neighbors (as does the Russian). These later film versions would try to go back past the family to recreate a community that perhaps the filmmakers and their viewers desired but felt themselves to be lacking. Nevertheless, each of these four films ends with a focus on the family as a microcosm of that community, or perhaps as a substitute for it. At the end of the Yiddish film, Tevye is looking forward to going to *Eretz Yisroel* (the Land of Israel), but, as in the text, it is unclear if or how he will get there. The English film accounts for each family member's destination; the community splits up, but families reunite or await their reunion in America. The Hebrew film reunites them as well, en route to the Land of Israel. And the Russian version expands the family metaphor even as its members are destroyed. The social, political, economic chaos is somewhat contained by its displacement onto the family. In comparison, the chaos of the family is merely unruly. It does not bring with it the proximate threat of extinction. The family becomes the site of struggle but also support, a place where conflict and resolution are more manageable than they are in society as a whole. There is some hope that the problems of the family can be addressed, encompassed, understood; those of society at large are *too* large. And, finally, whether in 1895, 1916, or 1939, or more recently, the resolution of familial—as opposed to social—conflict can at least be imagined. In the end, then, Sholem Aleichem does envision a welcoming destination, toward which, in their varied ways, these films follow him.

CHAPTER 3

Remembering Jews

TRANSLATING YIDDISH AFTER THE HOLOCAUST

> Nothing teaches more clearly that the world is not yet redeemed than
> the multiplicity of languages.
> —Franz Rosenzweig, *The Star of Redemption*

MANY years ago I got into trouble at an international Yiddish conference. My transgression? I suggested that Isaac Bashevis Singer wrote
primarily for an English-speaking audience and for those—Jews and non-Jews
alike—who were fairly remote from either the Eastern European world he pur-
ported to invoke or the immigrant Jewish American experience. A senior,
learned, distinguished scholar of Yiddish I deeply respected suggested that the
reason I was making this claim was that I had no personal understanding of
or access to the *shtetl* (small town), to *cheder* (Jewish elementary education), to
yeshiva (advanced Jewish religious and textual education), to Polish, to Warsaw,
to traditional religious life, to the political revolutions of the twentieth century,
to the seductive nature of secular knowledge and the newness of modern
romantic love. I had, in short, never known Isaac Bashevis Singer's milieu.

I replied, I am now sorry to say, in a rather petulant and certainly intimi-
dated way. I lamented that if attendance at a traditional Polish yeshiva and
rebellion from it were the requirements for the creation of Yiddish scholarship, then most of us in the room were automatically disqualified. I understood
this scholar—who will continue to remain nameless—to be putting me in my
place by invoking the three exclusionary Gs of Jewish culture: geography, generation, and gender. On the basis of these, he proclaimed that Yiddish culture

in its deepest (read: most worthwhile) sense was closed to me. I could not argue with this logic, which was, of course, its point. Indeed, I had not been there or done that: I had never set foot in Poland; I was born after the Second World War; and no yeshiva would ever have allowed me to study within its walls.

This incident encapsulates for me one of the major problems of translating Yiddish into English. What was at stake in this exchange had little to do with the literary reputation of Isaac Bashevis Singer, or Yitzhok Bashevis as he is known in Yiddish, and everything to do with the past, present, and future status of Yiddish and the culture of Eastern European and much of American Jewry.

More than raising questions about accuracy or knowledge or fidelity to a text, the very act of translation from Yiddish to English seems to hint, as I have been suggesting, at the end of a culture: replacing Yiddish words with English ones seems to suggest that Yiddish has no audience or future. Translation from Yiddish can feel like a capitulation to history. It implies that these texts will no longer be read by anyone in their original—that these texts, like their intended audience, will disappear. Translation becomes, potentially, a form of obliteration. The ongoing existence of Yiddish, in this context, can be understood as resistance, and translation as an act of collaboration in the destruction of a culture, a betrayal of the language in which it flourished and the millions who spoke it.

Yet a simultaneous and seemingly contradictory view of translation also exists. The cultural valence of Yiddish in today's world suggests that translation may be an act of *resistance* to history. Increasingly, everything one does with or in Yiddish—speaking, reading, writing, teaching, translation, scholarship— may be understood as a defiant gesture aimed at preserving the traces of a culture that underwent startling and dreadful transformations in the previous century. The arbiters of cultural politics demand that translators be faithful to the Yiddish originals if they are to avoid taking part in the obliteration of the culture they purport to know; translators, in turn, suggest that their work will turn the historical tide, not only preserving Yiddish culture, but helping it proliferate. In either case, however reluctant we may be to invoke it, the language of the Holocaust is pivotal to the discussion: as collaborators or resisters, Yiddish translators are inevitably measured by daunting standards.

One of the primary questions raised about Yiddish translation concerns its nature as a Jewish language. How can a Jewish language steeped in Jewish ritual and culture hope to be understood in non-Jewish languages? Bashevis once came to an event in his honor at YIVO (the Yiddish Research Institute in New York). He began to read a Yiddish story, and in the midst of it he stopped himself—as he was dramatically wont to do—and said the story was too difficult for his listeners to follow because we were unlikely to know the *loshn-koydesh*—the Hebrew and Aramaic—he was quoting or, in an echo of my anecdote, the religious world in which it existed. We were uneducated, too young, too American, too secular, many of us also too female. He switched to a more American and, he thought, therefore easier story. There are, indeed, obvious differences between Bashevis's invocation of "Rosh Hashanah" and an English reader's understanding of "the New Year," between "Tammuz" and "summer months," or "Shabbos Nakhamu" and "the Sabbath after the observance of the mourning day of Tisha B'av in which the Torah portion concerning consolation is read." There are similarly obvious differences between the term *non-Jews* and *goyim*, between *shabbos* or *shabbat* and *the Sabbath*. And it is the task of the translator to convey those differences. But Bashevis's lament—at YIVO and elsewhere—serves mainly to mystify and not to clarify. Despite excellent translations of his prose, Bashevis contributed to the mistaken notion that Yiddish is, by its nature and context, different from other languages.

The reputations of the heralded American Jewish writer, Isaac Bashevis Singer, and the Yiddish writer, Yitzhok Bashevis, are noteworthy in their differences. Until his ascension into the highest ranks of American literati, and even later, Bashevis was primarily known in Yiddish as the younger brother of the writer Israel Joshua Singer and as a storyteller with a disturbing penchant for describing Jews who transgressed: thieves, prostitutes, disreputable businessmen, corrupt rabbis, and men and women who thought their sexual orgies might hasten the coming of the messiah. Yitzhok Hersh Zynger (1904–1991) was born near Warsaw into a family whose members seemed to embody the defining Jewish struggles of the twentieth century. His oldest sibling, Hinde Ester (Esther Singer Kreitman), was widely regarded as the family hysteric, and her writing was rarely even acknowledged by her family; his brother Yisroel (I. J. Singer), two years younger than their sister and eleven years older than Yitzhok, would become a famous Yiddish writer long before Yitzhok; two sisters born between the brothers died in childhood; a younger brother, Moshe, the only one to remain within the family fold, followed his father into the rabbinate and died during the Second World War, along with their mother. The story of the domestic tensions caused by their mother's rationalist Judaism and their father's mystical enthusiasm is too familiar to be retold here, but these tensions were unquestionably founda-tional for the writer—each of the writers—who was to emerge.[1] To distin-guish himself from his brother, Yitzhok took their mother's name (Batsheva) when he began to publish, calling himself Bashevis: Batsheva's. He began writ-ing in Poland and made a reputation for himself as a proofreader, a journalist, and, finally, an acclaimed fiction writer, with the publication of *Der sotn in goray: A mayse fun fartsaytns* (Satan in Goray: A tale of former days) in 1935.[2] His first novel explored the faith and depravity that accompanied the after-math of the Chmelnicki pogroms in the seventeenth century and the false messiah, Sabbatai Zvi, who followed them. In the same year, Bashevis fol-lowed his brother to New York and entered a decade-long period of literary silence, writing essays and criticism until his reemergence as a short story writer at the end of World War II. With the appearance of his next novel, *Di Familye Moskat* (*The Family Moskat*) in 1950, the American Isaac Singer was born, heir not only to the fame of his older brother, who died in 1944, but, even more poignantly, to an Eastern European past many saw as having been recently decimated beyond imagination.[3] It was precisely his ability to imag-ine and depict it that made him famous.

Although Bashevis had been in New York for fifteen years by the time the English version of *The Family Moskat* appeared, he claimed to have learned English in the process of working on this project. In so doing, he also claimed to have made English his "second language."[4] The claim must be understood more as rhetorical flourish than as biographical fact. It erased his native Polish and Hebrew, as well as his own early translations from German into Yiddish. Despite this claim, of course, and despite the very extensive revi-sions he undertook, he never actually wrote in English. And, ironically, even if English were to be reckoned as a second language, its status must be con-sidered primary given the audience Singer increasingly addressed.[5] He was famous for working very closely with his translators, correcting them and his Yiddish originals, and making such extensive revisions of his work that com-parisons of the Yiddish and English versions of his stories and novels can reveal remarkably different texts, targeted to different audiences, responsive not only to the different cultures that Yiddish and English readers inhabit but also to the different cultural moments in which each version was produced.

The differences between the Yiddish and English versions of *The Family Moskat* establish a pattern that would be repeated for the next forty years of the author's life, and even beyond as posthumous works appear: Jewish reli-gious terms are erased or glossed, lengthy and often repetitive serialized novels are shortened, and whole episodes in the Yiddish may be eliminated in the English. Irving Saposnik's careful comparison of the two versions analyzes the creation of two different novels for different audiences.[6] Underscoring the English version's systematic exclusion of any reference to messianic faith, Saposnik argues that Bashevis found such belief inappropriate for his new American audience. The most dramatic difference between the two texts is that the Yiddish version is one chapter longer, concluding, as Saposnik convincingly illustrates, with further positive or at least ambivalent references to the faith denied in the English novel. Janet Hadda, Singer's biographer, reminds us that it was his publisher, Alfred A. Knopf (who was also his brother's publisher), who insisted on cutting this crucial last chapter and that Singer was unhappy about the change and left Knopf as a result.[7] Particularly at this early stage, it is often difficult to know which changes can be attributed to Singer, which to his translator, and which to his publishers. But it is certainly clear that each text was targeted for a different audience and that Bashevis learned not only English but also how to become Singer.

Three years after his English-language debut, Bashevis's now most anthologized story, "Gimpl tam," was translated by Saul Bellow and his reputation secured. By 1953, Bellow, who was more than a decade younger than Bashevis, had published two acclaimed novels, *Dangling Man* (1944) and *The Victim* (1947), and was completing another, *The Adventures of Augie March* (1953); he would go on to be awarded the Nobel Prize in Literature (1976) just two years before Bashevis himself received it. In most bibliographies of Bellow's work, "Gimpel the Fool" is the only translation credited to him, but there was at least one earlier, equally important, venture into Yiddish, this time in the opposite direction: from English to Yiddish. When Bellow and his close friend Isaac Rosenfeld were in their twenties, the two produced a Yiddish version of T. S. Eliot's "The Love Song of J. Alfred Prufrock" that became something of a legend in its own time and ours.[8] "Der shir hashirim fun Mendl Pumshtok" (The Song of Songs of Mendl Pumshtok) transforms Eliot's "one-night cheap hotels / And sawdust restaurants with oyster-shells" into a kosher restaurant where dirty bedding hangs and bedbugs do circle dances.[9] In Eliot's poem there is a room where "the women come and go / Talking of Michelangelo." In Bellow and Rosenfeld's version there are "*vayber*" (womenfolk) who speak of Marx and Lenin. The English poet's most resonant "I grow old . . . I grow old . . . / I shall wear the bottoms of my trousers rolled" becomes the Yiddish "*Ikh ver alt, ikh ver alt / Es vert mir in pupik kalt*" (I am getting old, I am getting old / My belly button is getting cold).

That "*pupik*" puts the poem—both poems—into perspective. It literally means "belly button" or "gizzard," certainly not the most appealing part of human or fowl. "*Pupik*" is the punch line for any number of Yiddish jokes and idioms that underscore the stupidity or uselessness of the subject. To call someone Moyshe Pupik (as, for example, Philip Roth knowingly does in *Operation Shylock*) is to call him a nobody, or worse: a nobody who you think thinks of himself as a somebody. To exclaim "*a dank dir in pupik*" (thanks to your belly button) is not to express gratitude but rather to say "thanks for absolutely nothing." Rosenberg and Bellow—neither of whom, it should be noted, had yet published any of the work that would make them famous a decade later—tell us exactly what they think of Eliot by invoking that *pupik*. He is overblown, he takes himself too seriously for no good reason, and his poetry can easily be deflated. Ruth R. Wisse views this poem as a kind of declaration of independence, a proclamation freeing American Jewish writers from the tyranny of English high modernism.[10] It points, as well, to the different cultural universes of English-language and Yiddish letters and to the ongoing, intimate, dialogues between them. Writers of Yiddish and English knew more about each other than is sometimes evident; they understood each other very well, revised each other, compelled their readers to see differently, to take mockery seriously and to mock seriousness. In its brilliant, parodic adaptation of Eliot's poem, "Der shir hashirim fun Mendl Pumshtok" should also help us put to rest the quest for fidelity to an original text.

Bellow's masterful translation of "Gimpl tam" ("Gimpel the Fool") seems animated by a different aesthetic and by dramatically different cultural and sociological motivations. The Yiddish story was first published in 1945 (in the Passover issue of the influential journal *Yidisher Kemfer*) and appeared in English in *Partisan Review* in 1953.[11] As with Wisse's claim for "Der shir hashirim fun Mendl Pumshtok," "Gimpel the Fool" has also been seen as a watershed in Jewish American letters. Sidra DeKoven Ezrahi suggests that the story "launched . . . a new phase in the representation of Jewish culture in America," one that sought to reclaim the Jewish past from which much of Jewish American culture had fled and to which it could no longer return.[12] It should give us pause to note that the Yiddish story first appeared at exactly the same time as the concentration camps of Europe were being liberated. We cannot separate the story, or its reception, from the events of the Holocaust, even though it gives no hint of the historical moment at which it was written. Still, those events cannot have been far from either writer's consciousness, and the story's critique of certain forms of Eastern European Jewish life is thus all the more remarkable. Prufrock was fair game for mockery, but Gimpel is not. Far from lampooning Bashevis's character, Bellow follows Bashevis in offering a modernist story of an enigmatic character in a dreadful situation, but he also makes that story and character less offensive to the sensibilities of an American reader. This desire to protect the non-Yiddish audience, to make things easier for those listeners or readers, recalls both the earlier anecdote I recounted about Bashevis at YIVO and the English version of *The Family Moskat*. It continued to be a defining characteristic of future translations of his work. In the English version of "Gimpel," Bellow retains the harsh critique of Gimpel's environs, but he removes some of the allusions that make perfect sense in Yiddish or that might give offense to the larger, non-Jewish world into which the story now enters. Oppressed both by his fellow townspeople and by his own naïveté, Gimpel suffers physical and psychological abuse. Orphaned, he is apprenticed to a baker and then married to a whore, who gives birth to a son four months later; her bastard children abuse him, beating and mocking him; twice, he returns home from work to find his wife in bed with another man. And yet he loves her and the children and clings to faith in God, in family structures, in everything he is told, even when he knows it cannot be true. Twenty years and six children later, his wife confesses on her deathbed, and Gimpel, finally angered by the deceptions perpetrated upon him by her and by the town as a whole, urinates into the dough that will feed them. At the last moment, though, he destroys the filthy bread, packs his meager beggar's sack, and leaves the town to await death. "Whatever may be there," he concludes in the final lines of the story, "it will be real, without complication, without ridicule, without deception. God be praised: there even Gimpel cannot be deceived" (*Vos s'zol dort nisht zayn, alts iz vor, on fardrey-enishn, on leytsones un shvindlen. Got tsu danken: dort kon men afilu Gimplen oykh nisht opnarn*).[13] Like the art of translation itself, the story must grapple with deception, with whether it is necessary, what is gained and lost by it.

Bellow's translation begins with a strong difference between the Yiddish and the English. Bashevis's "*Ikh bin Gimpl tam. Ikh halt mikh nisht far keyn nar*" becomes Bellow's "I am Gimpel the fool. I don't think myself a fool." The very last word of the Yiddish story will return us to the root word "*nar*" ("*opnarn*"), the fool who, Gimpel claims, will one day no longer be fooled and who, in truth, has been aware of deception all along. But the word "*tam*," with which the story begins, invokes, as Chone Shmeruk has noted, both the four sons of the Passover story (one of whom is a *tam*, a "simple one") and a story by Rabbi Nachman of Bratslav about a wise man and a simple one; a *nar* is simply a fool, and the story distinguishes the two quite clearly. The *tam* is a simple man but not a simpleton.[14] Gimpel is actually claiming to be no fool at all. Erasing the crucial distinction between *tam* and *nar*, Bellow elides the folkloric and religious resonances of *tam* as well as the numerous linguistic derivations from *nar*.[15] *Tam* suggests "innocence" and is a Hebrew-derived Yiddish word, no doubt of the kind that Bashevis did not trust his youthful YIVO audience to understand. Rather than regard this translation as an error, however, we should consider the alternatives Bellow might have chosen. The most faithful translation of Bashevis's "Gimpl tam" would have been "Gimpel the Simple," surely an infelicitous choice for an English writer or reader.[16] That literal translation, indeed, might have given the story something of the mocking effect produced for the T. S. Eliot translation, but the translation of "Gimpel tam" strives successfully for exactly the opposite effect: to ennoble both Gimpel and the culture for which he now stands. Bellow eschews, as well, English synonyms such as "Gimpel the Innocent" or "Gimpel the Naive" as plausible translations of "Gimpl tam," each of them suggesting somewhat different views of Gimpel's character than the view Bellow chose when he called the story "Gimpel the Fool." Instead of the *tam* of Jewish lore, we encounter the fool of other traditions and intertexts. Is this the fool who speaks truth? The English, but not the Yiddish, hints at the "holy fool" of Shakespearean drama, of Dostoyevsky's *The Idiot*, even of Christian tradition where rejection of the world and *imitatio dei* may lead one to be mocked, but it contains a much higher truth, suggesting (as does Paul in Corinthians) that foolishness is its own kind of divinity.[17] There is, of course, no lack of fools in Jewish lore, as is abundantly clear in the many folktales about the fools who live in the town of Chelm or, indeed, the many synonyms for "fool" that Bashevis gives us at the beginning of the story. But those fools are, for the most part, hapless; there is little wisdom concealed beneath their folly; they inspire derision or compassion but not admiration; they do not know how to live in this world, and it is not clear that their foolishness will be rewarded in the next. Bashevis does not call Gimpel a *shlimazl* or *schlemiel* and thus avoids making him the butt of bad jokes and even worse luck.[18]

The *"vor"* in the story's final line (in the world to come *"alts iz vor"*) is rendered by Bellow as "real," but it might just as easily have been understood as "true." Invoking different literary traditions, both Bellow and Bashevis leave deliberately unclear what reality or truth Gimpel will encounter after death. The Yiddish story may offer us some hope for reward in the "real" or "true" world to come, but it is an uncertain reward, made all the more ambiguous by Gimpel's inability to name or even imagine it. The English story is rather less ambiguous, however, precisely because it is framed in the title's allusion to a different kind of fool, one whose reward has already been anticipated. Naomi Seidman, who has written most profoundly about the Jewish and Christian differences revealed in translation, suggests that Gimpel should not be understood as the holy fool. "Gimpel, from beginning to end, somehow knows he is being fooled, and his character is made considerably less saintly by a barely suppressed rage that finally does erupt," she writes, reminding us, as well, that he gives "his" children his worldly goods but then leaves them without another thought.[19]

The confusion about the holy fool directs our attention to another significant difference between the Yiddish story and Bellow's translation, a difference that also points to the diverse audiences and cultural orbits they address. The most profound change made in the English version lies not in the confusion about how to understand the fool but rather in an erasure, to which a number of scholars have called attention. Janet Hadda highlights Bellow's omission of "the overt anti-Christian references contained in the Yiddish original," and Seidman goes on to enumerate some of them.[20] References to *shiksas* and *goyim*—non-Jewish women and people—are neutralized, no doubt because such words have made their way into English usage and are generally understood to be offensive. But, as Seidman points out, the omission of an entire Yiddish sentence requires another explanation. There is a Yiddish sentence that follows the incredible story Gimpel's wife tells him to explain how "their" son was born only seventeen weeks after their wedding: she claims to resemble her grandmother, to whom the same thing happened. Then a teacher, citing the Talmud, convinces Gimpel that even Adam and Eve had a similar experience: "Two they went up to bed, and four they descended. There isn't a woman in the world who is not the granddaughter of Eve."[21] Seidman cites the Yiddish line that concludes this episode in the story—"*Ot zogt men dokh, az s'yoyzel hot in gantsn keyn tatn nisht gehat*"—and translates it as "After all, they say that Yoyzl didn't have a father at all." Yoyzl, as she points out, is a diminutive for Jesus.[22] It is also one of the names Jews traditionally used in a derogatory manner, a way of containing the danger posed by the figure of Jesus. The name is also preceded in this sentence by the definite article "*dos*" (in the contraction "*s'yoyzel*"), thus rendering it "the" or "that" Yoyzl. All this is perfectly understood and grammatically acceptable in Yiddish, but it also underscores the distancing and insult in the use of "Yoyzl." Yiddish speakers add that article to various allusions to Jesus (as in *s'yoyzl* or *s'getsel*—literally "that little god" or, more pointedly, "that idol") to show their distance from any such belief and their disdain for it. ("*Nisht geshtoygn, nisht gefloygn*"—"didn't rise, didn't fly"—invoked earlier [see chapter 1], employs a similar strategy.) Surely, Bashevis seems to tell us, no one—not even Gimpel—could believe that story about Jesus's paternity. Bashevis goes over Gimpel's head here to address his Yiddish readers, who will unquestionably see the foolishness in Christian beliefs such as miraculous fatherhood or virgin birth. Had Bellow translated the line, he could not have relied on his English readers having a similar response or sharing a knowing smirk over that particular insider perspective.[23]

We cannot be certain whether it was Bellow, the English-language novelist, or Eliezer Greenberg, the Yiddish poet, who censored the line. Greenberg may well be the unsung hero of Yiddish-to-English translation. He would become familiar to American audiences for his collaboration with Irving Howe on anthologies of translated Yiddish prose and poetry (the first of them, *A Treasury of Yiddish Stories*, appeared the same year as "Gimpel the Fool"), but he was already well known as a Yiddish poet and critic. Hadda credits him with convincing the initially reluctant Bellow to translate "Gimpl tam" and with offering his help in the enterprise. Bellow was a fluent Yiddish speaker but was apparently less proficient as a reader, and so Greenberg commuted from New York to Princeton in order to read the Yiddish story aloud to Bellow, who typed the English as he was hearing the Yiddish.[24] One or both of them (or perhaps Bashevis himself?) showed an exaggerated, perhaps overly anxious, attention to the supposed sensibilities of the non-Jewish reader. In alluding to the holy fool and erasing the anti-Christian suggestions, the English story potentially turns "Gimpl tam" on its head, leaving us with a universal, sympathetic message of the faith that ennobles folly. That inversion is a central, repeated trope in the movement from Yiddish into English. What is lost in even so consummate a translation as Bellow's is context and the intimacy of being an insider among one's own. The English is a little too attentive to its imagined reader, too focused on reaching as wide an audience as possible, too concerned about giving offense, and perhaps too polite as well. Bashevis never seemed to worry about any of that in Yiddish, and in this, as in other ways I consider below, he was freer and often even bolder than Singer's stories might suggest.

George Steiner offers a discerning comment that may be applied to Singer. Referring to those writers who have translated or collaborated on the translation of their own works, Steiner observes that when an author significantly recasts a text in the act of rendering it in another language, he or she may produce "a text which is, in many respects, indispensable to the original."[25] There are, Steiner reminds us, original texts to which we no longer turn because "the translation is of a higher magnitude." Steiner calls such extraordinarily successful translation "betrayal by augment," a term we might usefully apply to Singer's own collaborative translation efforts and his privileging of the English texts.[26] Neither a view of Singer's English stories as secondary and derivative versions of Bashevis's Yiddish nor a view of them as edited improvements on novels that are often exceedingly repetitive and meandering seems apt. Rather, the Yiddish and English texts comment on each other, the latter reworking and sometimes differing with, sometimes completing, the ideational and imaginative work of the former. The English clarifies the Yiddish, but for a growing audience it also replaces the Yiddish as the definitive text. This is typical of the history of Yiddish literature in America, but Singer is remarkable among Yiddish writers in the extent to which he contributes to and validates this usurpation of Yiddish by English even as he suggests a different model, one that allows for the "second original" of the second language.

Critics and scholars may be more concerned with the differences between the Yiddish and English texts than Singer or his translators were. Singer had little tolerance for the work of literary critics, and he would most likely have been dismissive of the scholarly interest in comparing his works.[27] In creating his "second originals" for a different audience he was primarily concerned with the new context and what he believed appropriate to it. His memoir, *In My Father's Court*, offers a provocative indication of what might have inspired some of these changes and the direction they took.[28] When "In mayn foters bezdn-shtub" appeared in the *Forverts* in 1955, it was signed by the journalistic pseudonym Yitzhok Varshavsky. By then, the writer was already famous in both Yiddish and English. He was the only survivor of his family, the final interpreter of his own family romance and of the Eastern European world on which it had been staged. A decade later, the book appeared in English, and the differences between the two versions are remarkable. His original, Yiddish text contains eleven chapters that are omitted in the English version, and the remaining English chapters change the sequence of the Yiddish without offering any clear chronological or thematic ordering of events.[29]

Despite the prevalent critical wisdom that points to Bashevis's willingness to depict Eastern European life in often quite literally naked terms, even exaggerating its perversions and ugliness, this memoir suggests that he was more guarded in English than in Yiddish. While leaving a clear impression of the corruption and perversity that exist amid the devout, traditional Jews of Warsaw, Bashevis excises some of the most unsavory characters of the Yiddish text. He seems most concerned with erasing those scenes that reflect particularly badly on his parents. His father's extraordinary innocence about the world, his mother's unsentimental rationalism, and their less than ideal life together are central to many of these scenes. In the Yiddish but not the English text, for example, he tells of the times when his father spent much-needed family money to publish his own scholarly books rather than to provide a dowry for his daughter (chap. 32). Or he discusses his father's naive assertion that anarchists must be messianic Jews because both true believers reject governmental authority and material wealth (chap. 31). Here and elsewhere, the mighty power of translation enables Bashevis to create a different set of decorums for Yiddish and English audiences. The latter, more likely to romanticize the traditional world, is given an idealized core of family reminiscences, one that privileges the view of a people "prepared to suffer in the name of spiritual purity" (*In My Father's Court* [English], 230), while ignoring the less savory characteristics of those people.

Another illustration of the deliberate changes Bashevis wrote into this narrative concerns the depiction of his sister and mother. Devoting a chapter of his memoir to their problematic relationship, Bashevis observes about his emotionally volatile sibling: "*Zi hot khoyshed geven az di mame hot zi nisht lib. Dos iz nisht geven emes, ober s'iz emes az di mame hot zi nisht gekont fartrogn*" (*Mayn tatns bezdn-shtub*, 158). The published English translation distorts this forceful statement, rendering it as "my sister suspected my mother of not loving her, which was untrue, but actually they were incompatible" (*In My Father's Court*, 145). A more faithful translation would read: "She suspected that my mother didn't love her. That was untrue, but it is true that my mother couldn't bear her." On the further reflection afforded Singer by revision and translation into English, he represses this less discreet assessment of the relationship between Batsheva Singer and her daughter. Once again, such changes should be attributed not to a weak translation or to error but rather to the perspective the author assumes at a different time and with a different audience. Singer appears less *heymish* (at home, one of "us") in the English version, more like a guest in someone else's home who is overly conscious of social niceties and appearances.

His sister's work offers an earlier example of the editing and rethinking that may accompany translation and, more emphatically, of the differences the Second World War seemed to demand of Yiddish writers. In her thinly veiled autobiographical novel, *Der sheydim tants* (*The Dance of the Demons*; 1936), Esther Singer Kreitman offers a remarkably similar view of the relationship between mother and daughter. In the English text, her protagonist, Deborah, laments that she is "so little thought of by her mother."[30] But in Yiddish, she thinks "*zi gefelt nisht der muter*" ("she is not pleasing to her mother" or, simply, "her mother doesn't like her").[31] First written in 1936, the novel was translated by Kreitman's son, Maurice Carr, ten years later. I have speculated elsewhere that Kreitman may well have had a great deal of influence over her son in the translation process; her command of English was excellent, and she had translated from English into Yiddish.[32] One or both of them certainly edited the Yiddish text, no doubt because the perspective of a Yiddish novel written in 1936 seemed no longer appropriate for an English novel produced in 1946.[33] Her brother Yitzhok would make almost identical changes in his texts. I am suggesting not that he learned his translation techniques from his older sister—certainly he would never have acknowledged that even if it were the case—but that the conditions and motivations we see at work in translations of their texts were strikingly, even uncannily, similar. Kreitman's novel is made accessible to a British postwar readership by substituting Cockney inflection for the Warsaw Yiddish of the original. Her allusions to Talmudic or biblical texts become, in English, intertextual references to Dickens or other writers. Some attention is paid to the explanation of Jewish ritual and religion. All of this is familiar to us (minus the Cockney!) from her brother's texts. And, as her brother would soon learn to do, the English version renders "*goyim un goyes*," or the more pejorative "*shkotsim un shikselekh*," into the utterly neutral "men and women" or "youths." The need to educate an English audience and to redeem some part of the now decimated Eastern European past is felt in every chapter of this English novel, which begins with an invocation of a Sabbath celebration not found in the original and goes on to soften the depiction of the mismatched parents. In *Der sheydim tants*, Kreitman describes a home in which may be found everything "except anything at all redolent of home" (*akhuts abisl azoyns, vos zol shmekn mit heym*).[34] In the English, such passages are simply omitted, moderating a bit the unremittingly bleak view of the earlier text. It is a protective gesture, and it may also help explain the increased focus in *Deborah* on the protagonist's role in the family and especially on her psyche. As we saw in Sholem Aleichem's *Tevye*, there is some possibility for addressing, perhaps even remedying, psychological distress, individual trauma, and childhood unhappiness. There is, in 1946, no future change to be imagined in the world of Eastern European Jewry. The desire to tear down that world has become a reality, and there must be a retreat from expressing it too forcefully.

By the time Singer won the Nobel Prize, there was no longer any doubt that he had become the voice of Yiddish and of Eastern European Jewry by universalizing its experience. He won the award, as the Prize Committee noted, "for his impassioned narrative art which, with roots in a Polish-Jewish cultural tradition, brings universal human conditions to life."[35] His acceptance speech offers the most telling example of his ongoing mystification of Yiddish.

Before beginning his formal presentation, Singer said that upon hearing of the award he decided "to speak a little in Yiddish for this distinguished audience because no one has ever spoken Yiddish here in this hall. And only God knows if someone is going to speak Yiddish here again." The audience applauded and laughed.[36] The laughter should give us pause. Tongue in cheek, Singer creates a community of like-minded insiders who know that Yiddish, of course, has never been a fit vehicle for the Nobel (until now), that it is laughable to think it could have been spoken among such distinguished people or in those hallowed halls. To say "Yiddish" is to invite laughter. He goes on to say that he knows they will not understand his Yiddish, but he will be brief and continue in English. Yiddish, then, is both funny and incomprehensible to these cultured people. At the same time, however, Singer may be enjoying the joke at the expense not of Yiddish but of the audience itself, whose members might think that they are too refined for such a folksy language. Singer enchants his audience, giving them an Old World charmer who laughs with them, but who may also be laughing at them. Not incidentally, of course, he makes himself the first and last Yiddish laureate. But just as Rosenfeld and Bellow put Eliot in his place, Singer also puts Yiddish in its place: as the newly canonized, universally recognized language of modern literature, impossible to ignore and, as he goes on to make clear, impossible to mock.

The published Yiddish reads as follows:

דער גרויסער כבוד וואָס די שוועדיקע אַקאַדעמיע האָט מיר אָנגעטאָן איז אויך
אַן אָנערקענונג פֿון אידיש—אַ שפּראַך פֿון גלות, אָן אַ לאַנד, אָן גרענעצן, נישט
אונטערגעשטיצט פֿון קיין שום רעגירונג; אַ שפּראַך וואָס פֿאַרמאָגט כמעט נישט קיין
ווערטער פֿון וואָפֿן, אַמוניציע, מיליטערישע איבונגען און טאַקטיק; אַ לשון וואָס איז

געוואָרן פֿאַראַכטעט סאי פֿון גוײם און סאי פֿון רוב עמאַנציפּירטע אידן. דער אמת איז,
אַז וואָס די גרױסע רעליגיעס האָבן געפּרעדיקט האָבן די אידן אין געטאָ פּראַקטיצירט.
זײ האָבן נישט געהאַט קײן גרעסערע פֿרײד װי לערנען װעגן מענטשן און מענטשלעכע
באַציאונגען װאָס זײ האָבן אָנגערופֿן תורה, תלמוד, מוסר, קבלה. די געטאָ איז געװען
נישט בלױז אַן אָרט פֿון אַנטרירונג פֿאַר אַ פֿאַרפֿאָלגטער מינאָריטעט, נאָר אױך אַ
גרױסער עקספּערימענט אין שלום, זעלבסט־דיסציפּלין און הומאַניזם. רעשטלעך
דערפֿון עקזיסטירן ביז הײַנט צו טאָג, נישט געקוקט אױף דער גאַנצער ברוטאַליטעט
װאָס רינגלט זײ אַרום.[37]

The published English:

The high honor bestowed upon me by the Swedish Academy is also a recognition of the Yiddish language—a language of exile, without a land, without
frontiers, not supported by any government, a language which possesses no
words for weapons, ammunition, military exercises, war tactics; a language
that was despised by both gentiles and emancipated Jews. The truth is that
what the great religions preached, the Yiddish-speaking people of the ghettos practiced day in and day out. They were the people of The Book in the
truest sense of the word. They knew of no greater joy than the study of man
and human relations, which they called Torah, Talmud, Mussar, Cabala. The
ghetto was not only a place of refuge for a persecuted minority but a great
experiment in peace, in self-discipline and in humanism. As such it still
exists and refuses to give up in spite of all the brutality that surrounds it.[38]

But when he was standing on the Stockholm stage, Singer only spoke the
Yiddish paragraph, without translating it into English. Instead, he continued
his speech by beginning it again, repeating his greetings to his distinguished
hosts and listeners and proceeding in English, offsetting this strange sound
of the foreign Yiddish even further. In his rich and flawless Yiddish, Singer
claims that the language has no words for weapons or war, dismissing the
very words he is uttering as being entirely alien to that "Polish-Jewish cultural tradition" the Academy is honoring. And then he refrains from translating his Yiddish remarks. His point is not a linguistic but a cultural one. He
mythologizes Yiddish, offering a view of its essentially peaceful and exalted
nature, and, more pointedly, he commemorates and ennobles the speakers
who were innocent of the political, nationalist, racist obscenities of the twentieth century to which they were subject.
In effect, Bashevis's essentializing notions about Yiddish and Jewish cul-

ture lament—as did that distinguished scholar about whom I began this chapter—the loss of an ideal reader, who, theoretically and certainly literally, does not exist. Those who now read and interpret and find meaning in Singer's texts are, without doubt, quite different from this ideal and increasingly idealized reader; however, Singer certainly knew he was writing for this particular interpretive community, one that had not been to cheder, or lived on the streets where Yiddish lived, or prayed in or fled the prayer houses and study houses of Poland. At least since the 1950s, Singer was addressing not those who had once experienced the culture he invoked but, rather, precisely those who had not. He is so widely read not because he renders the familiar but because—whether through demons or imps or sexual license or realistic descriptions of the past—he emphasizes the strange and unfamiliar. His stories speak authoritatively to readers who are so far removed from the Eastern European world he describes that they have come to long for it, to reify it.

Singer himself was fond of insisting that he never wrote with any reader in mind. (Walter Benjamin and other theorists might have applauded this claim.) "[I]f I did remember while I was writing that some of my readers were dying and others were not being born to replace them, it might have some influence on me. Writers, as a rule, don't think about their readers while they write. As a matter of fact, thinking about the reader is a terrible pitfall for a writer," he said in an interview. He went on to insist: "I take great care not to think about the reader in English or French or any other language. Nothing can spoil a writer more than writing for the translator. He must feel that he writes for people who know everything he knows—not for the stranger."[39] Still, despite these pronouncements, it is hard to imagine that he was indifferent to the harsh Yiddish criticism to which he was subject or to his adoring English critics who were to influence his readership. The Nobel Prize was one result of the latter. Irving Howe expressed the former succinctly when he wrote: "That Singer has always been regarded with some uneasiness in the Yiddish literary world is hardly a secret."[40] Singer's claim to ignoring his readers in the creative process was disingenuous at best. In interviews and in writing, he took positions that seem to contradict this claim to authorial innocence. He was unhappy about the translation follies of his youth when he rendered German, Polish, and Hebrew texts into Yiddish, but, as he later lamented, "didn't work as hard on them as I should have."[41] In the 1930s, Bashevis translated the work of the Norwegian writer Knut Hamsun, via the German, thus foreshadowing what would become the common practice of translating his own works through an intermediary language—in his case, English—rather than the original.[42] Later, he was insistent about his role in the translation process and the changes he introduced on behalf of the English reader. He was notoriously dissatisfied with most of his translators, changing them frequently, publicly regretting the necessary losses a writer faced in translation, and asserting that the editorial process was central to the process of translation. "There isn't such a thing as a good translator. The best translators make the worst mistakes," he wrote.[43] As he was fond of reminding his readers: "For years I worked together with the translators on *The Family Moskat.* . . . Since that time I have taken part in the translation of every one of my books. I think only in this way can a translation come out bearable. I say 'bearable,' because you know just as much as I do that writers inevitably lose a great deal in translation."[44] (Whatever we may believe his works may have lost, this writer, it must be acknowledged, actually gained a great deal—readers, fame, money—in translation.) Ruth Whitman expressed some frustration with Singer's relationship to her and other translators. His "method of working," she wrote, "is to translate with his translator, phrase by phrase, sentence by sentence," and she goes on to cite an interview in the *National Jewish Monthly* in which Singer said: "I go through my writings again and again while I edit the translation and work with the translator, and I see the defects of my writing while I am doing this."[45] He could claim the English version of his work as "a second original" precisely because his revisions were typically so extensive.[46] It is no wonder that he worked so closely with his translators since he correctly understood his literary reputation and future to rest on the English texts they helped him produce.

Singer's texts in translation have certainly entered into the canon of Jewish literature in America and of American literature and world literature. They have also, as we have seen, been radically transformed in the process. Perhaps the very best example of that is a story that became the award-winning film *Yentl.* This time, the translation is not only from Yiddish into English but from short story into film, from prose into song, and from Bashevis into Singer and then into Barbra Streisand. Bashevis originally published "Yentl der yeshive-bokher" in 1963. It was translated into English, as usual, with Singer's helpful hand, and published in 1962, even before the Yiddish version appeared in print, as "Yentl the Yeshiva Boy: A Story." It was adapted for the stage in the 1970s and then for the screen in 1983.[47] The *gilgulim*—the various incarnations—of *Yentl* underscore the importance of considering the intended or imagined audience for Singer's works. Singer hated the film and wrote a harsh mock-review in the form of a self-interview for the *New York Times*.[48] His own screenplay was rejected by Streisand and replaced by one of her devising, which he criticized mercilessly. He had nothing to do with the film and thus bears no responsibility for the Americanization of his story. But it is another intriguing vision of what can happen when a work is "translated" and of the many hands whose imprint it bears.

The story is familiar to American moviegoers. It is considered to have been inspired by the plight of Bashevis's sister, Hinde Ester. Yentl poses as a young man, is therefore able to study Jewish texts, falls in love with another student, but, still pretending to be male, marries another young woman. The film ends, much like *Fiddler on the Roof* but unlike Singer's story, en route to America, the golden land where anything is possible. In America, we are told, there is even happiness for a girl who has lived as a boy, loved a boy, married a girl, and yearns to study.

There are several fascinating details in the film's final minutes. For example, we see a *sefer*—a sacred book—that is facing the viewing audience rather than its supposed reader. We cannot know if it is a boy or girl reading the book, but we certainly do not see the traditional skullcap that we would expect to see on a male's head. Nor are any of the headcoverings of the other men and women on the ship to America anything like that of the figure on whom the camera focuses. The brown cap covering the figure's hair and the simple jacket buttoned high could belong to anyone; it is unclear whether that figure is male or female until we hear the voice. (Although, it should be noted, it is difficult to imagine that anyone watching the film ever forgets that Barbra Streisand is most definitely not a man!) The voice we hear is singing "Papa, Can You Hear Me?"—a song that invokes Yentl's father in a film that is dedicated to Streisand's own father and that is meant to invoke (to adapt Irving Howe's famous title) the "World of [All of] Our Fathers."

At the film's end, however, we finally see her in a skirt belting out her song of opportunity. Throughout the film, we have been aware that this is a girl in men's clothing. Streisand is at some pains to underscore Yentl's femininity, to show us her dawning love for a man who finally awakens within her the womanly desires she has long suppressed. Her "true nature" is to be free, to go and do as she wishes. She is a feminist and an American, two categories remote indeed from Bashevis's aesthetic or philosophical perspective. She may want to be free, to sail the high seas en route to a new land, but by film's end she has also gone back to her "true" self: the girl who carries the Old

World with her (as does Tevye in *Fiddler on the Roof*) and whose Papa (again, like the fiddler) is a bridge to the New World.

"What would Yentl have done in America?" Singer mockingly asked in his review. "Worked in a sweatshop 12 hours a day . . .? Would she try to marry a salesman in New York, move to the Bronx or to Brooklyn and rent an apartment with an ice box and a dumbwaiter?"[49] In deflating the movie in this way, he reasserts the protagonist's desire to learn above all else. And he insists on the fact that there were plenty of yeshivas in Poland or Lithuania where she could have studied if she continued to dress in drag.

Bashevis's story is radically different from this film. In Bashevis's Yiddish version, Yentl retains the identity of Anshel, the young man she has become in the story, rejecting the love of Avigdor, the study partner with whom she has fallen in love, to whom she has revealed herself, and who now imagines a life with the friend he, too, has come to love. "Yentl der yeshive-bokher" is a story about desire and transgression and identity. It includes all the elements of a sensational and controversial Bashevis story: cross-dressing, androgyny, homoerotic desire between two apparent men and between two women, and homosexual love. The film, not surprisingly, only hints at these elements and keeps very clear the distinctions between male and female. The original Bashevis story, in contrast, insists on—we could even say revels in— blurring those distinctions.[50]

There are, however, some telling differences even between the Yiddish and English written texts. For the most part, the English "Yentl" adheres closely to the original. But a few contrary examples are illuminating. In Bashevis's Yiddish, for example, as Anshel (Yentl) is developing the plan to marry Hadass, he writes:

> Only then did Anshel remember that it was Avigdor who had wanted her to marry Hadass. From her confusion, a plan emerged: she would exact vengeance for Avigdor, and at the same time, through Hadass, draw him closer to herself. Hadass was a virgin: what did she know about men? A girl like that could be deceived for a long time. To be sure, Anshel too was a virgin, but she knew a lot about such matters from the Gemara and from hearing men talk. Anshel was seized by both fear and glee, as a person is who is planning to deceive the whole community. She remembered the saying: "The public are fools." She stood up and said aloud: "Now I'll really start something."
>
> That night Anshel didn't sleep a wink. Every few minutes she got up for

a drink of water. <u>Her</u> throat was parched, <u>her</u> forehead burned. <u>Her</u> brain
worked away feverishly of its own volition. A quarrel seemed to be going on
inside <u>her</u>. <u>Her</u> stomach throbbed and her knees ached. It was as if <u>she</u> had
sealed a pact with Satan, the Evil One who plays tricks on human beings,
who sets stumbling blocks and traps in their paths. By the time Anshel fell
asleep, it was morning. <u>She</u> awoke more exhausted than before. But <u>she</u>
could not go on sleeping on the bench at the widow's. With an effort <u>she</u>
rose and, taking the bag that held <u>her</u> phylacteries, set out for the study
house. On the way, whom should <u>she</u> meet but Hadass's father. Anshel bade
him a respectful good morning and received a friendly greeting in return.

עֶר הָאָט זיך ערשט איצט דערמאָנט אַז אַבֿיגדור הָאָט <u>אים</u> גערָאטן <u>עֶר</u> זָאל ווערן אַ
חתן מיט דער הדסן. פֿון הינטער דער גאָנצער צעמישטקייט הָאָט זיך אויסגעשיילט אַ
פּלאַן: צו נעמען נקמה אָן אַבֿיגדורן און אים צוציען צו זיך, וויֵיל עֶר וועט די הדסן קיין
מָאל נישט פֿאַרגעסן. די הדס איז אַ כשרה בתולה, —ווָאס ווייסט זי פֿון מאַנסלייט?
מ'קָאן אַזָא אַיינע לאַנג אַ נאַרן. צווָאר, <u>זי, יענטל</u>, איז אויך אַ בתולה, אָבער <u>זי ווייסט</u> אַ סך
פֿון דער גמרא און פֿון צוהערן זיך צו די מאַנסבילישע שמועסן. אַ פֿחד הָאָט אָנגענומען
אַנשלען און די פֿרייד פֿון יענע ווָאס גרייט זיך אָפּצונאַרן קהל. <u>עֶר</u> הָאָט זיך דערמאָנט
דאָס ווערטל: דער עולם איז אַ גולם. <u>עֶר</u> הָאָט זיך אויפֿגעשטעלט און אַ זָאג געטאָן:
. . . !איכ'ל שוין פֿאַרקאָכן יענע קאָשע—

יענע נאַכט איז אַנשל נישט געשלאָפֿן קיין אויגנבליק. ס'הָאָט <u>אים</u> געטריקנט דער
דאָרשט און <u>עֶר</u> איז יעדעס מָאל אַראָפּ צום וואַסער טָאן אַ טרונק. דער שטערן איז
<u>אים</u> געווען הייס. די געהירן אין שיידל הָאָבן געאַרבעט אויף אייגענער אחריות. עמיץ
הָאָט אין <u>אים</u> גערעדט און געענטפֿערט. אין בויך הָאָט <u>אים</u> געקלעמט. די קני הָאָבן
גערעבאָכן וויִ אין אַ היצשלאַפֿקייט. <u>עֶר</u> הָאָט וויִ געשלאָסן אַ בונד מיט דעם יצר־הרע,
דעם שטן ווָאס נאַרט אָפּ מענטשן, לייגט זיי אונטער שטרויכלשטיינער, פֿאַרוועבט זיי
אין שאַלקהאַפֿטיקע געוועבן. ערשט אין דער פֿרי איז אַנשל אַיינגעשלאָפֿן אַ שווערן
שלאָף. <u>עֶר</u> איז אויפֿגעקומען מידער וויִ <u>עֶר</u> הָאָט זיך געלייגט. <u>עֶר</u> הָאָט נישט געקאָנט
בלייבן ליגן ביַי דער אַלמנה אין באַנקבעטל און <u>עֶר</u> הָאָט זיך געטאָן אַ כּוח אויפֿצושטיין.
<u>עֶר</u> איז אַוועק אין בית־מדרש מיט דעם תּפֿילין־זעקל. אין גאַ הָאָט <u>עֶר</u> באַגעגנט אַלטער
ווישקָאווער, אים צוגעטראָגן דעם גוט־מאָרגן און יענער הָאָט <u>אים</u> אָפּגעענטפֿערט
פֿריינדלעך.51

Consider the lines in which Anshel (Yentl) thinks about Hadass's
innocence:

Hadass was a virgin: what did she know about men? A girl like that could
be deceived for a long time. To be sure, Anshel too was a virgin, but she

knew a lot about such matters from the Gemara and from hearing men talk. Anshel was seized by both fear and glee, as a person is who is planning to deceive the whole community. She remembered the saying: "The public are fools."

"*Der oylem iz a goylem*"—literally "people are golems," meaning that they are clay figures who can't think for themselves—is not quite the same as "the public are fools"—another sign of the way fools have dogged Singer's English texts. But what is most significant here is the movement from "*zi, Yentl, iz oykh a besula*" to "Anshel too was a virgin," from "*Er hot zikh dermont . . .*" to "She remembered . . ." rather than "He remembered." In Yiddish, the text reminds us that it is Yentl who is a virgin, not, as the English would have it, Anshel. But even more striking is the change of pronoun. The English refers to Anshel as "she" or "her," reminding us at every turn of just who this character is—that the person who has assumed a male name is still a female. Throughout this passage and others like it, the English text keeps on reminding us that Anshel is really a woman merely posing as a man. In the Yiddish text her character is completely transformed, right down to the use of male pronouns ("*er*," "*im*"); in Yiddish she becomes that man.

That difference is consistent throughout, as the underlined words above dramatically illustrate. Where the Yiddish says "*Anshel iz nisht geshlofn vayl s'hot IM getriknt der dorsht un ER iz yedes mol arop tsum vaser*" (emphasis mine), the English says "Anshel didn't sleep a wink. Every few minutes she [not *er* (he)] got up for a drink of water. Her [not *zayn* (his)] throat was parched." Like our earlier examples, this difference must be considered not error or editorial license but rather a deliberate change, one in which Singer would most likely have had considerable say. Yentl's movements in Yiddish are from female to female-posing-as-male to ambiguously male; in English, she remains unambiguously female. These transformations are not that different from the one we have noted in the writer's own name. Bashevis, the man who assumed his mother's name but kept his first name, combined male and female. But in English he publishes, unambiguously, as Isaac Singer. He becomes a writer whose masculinity is clearly asserted to a new audience.

For a very different example of these movements between genders, we turn to the scene of the couple's wedding night. In Streisand's movie, the wedding is not consummated. Anshel/Yentl has the unsuspecting Hadass drink herself into a stupor. When the bedsheets are inspected for the signs of blood that would indicate that Hadass is no longer a virgin, what is found on them the next morning is the wine Anshel/Yentl has spilled in order to deceive the community.

Compare the Yiddish and English texts:

At daybreak, Anshel's mother-in-law and her band descended upon the marriage chamber and tore the bedsheets from beneath Hadass to make sure the marriage had been consummated. When traces of blood were discovered, the company grew merry and began kissing and congratulating the bride. Then, brandishing the sheet, they flocked outside and danced a kosher dance in the newly fallen snow. Anshel had found a way to deflower the bride. Hadass in her innocence was unaware that things weren't quite as they should have been. She was already in love with Anshel. It is commanded that the bride and groom remain apart for seven days after the first intercourse. The next day Anshel and Avigdor took up the study of the Tractate on Menstruous Women. When the other men had departed and the two were left to themselves in the synagogue, <u>Avigdor shyly questioned Anshel about his night with Hadass.</u> Anshel gratified his curiosity and they whispered together until nightfall.

פֿאַר טאָג זענען די מחותּנתטעס און זייערע קומעס אַרײַנגעפֿאַלן צו חתן-כּלה אין
שלאָפֿשטוב און אָפּגעריסן פֿון אונטער הדסן דאָס לײלעך זיך איבערצוצײַגן צי דער
מאַן האָט זיך מיט איר ס'באַהאָפֿטן. זײ האָבן געפֿונען אױפֿן לײלעך פֿלעקן פֿון בלוט און
דאָס געזינדל איז געװאָרן אָפֿגערדיק. זײ האָבן געקושט די כּלה און איר געװוּנטשן
מזל-טובֿ, דערנאָך זענען זײ אַרױס מיט דעם לײלעך אין דרױסן און געטאַנצט דערמיט
אַ כּשר-טאַנץ אין פֿריש-אָנגעפֿאַלענעם שניי. אַנשל האָט געהאַט געפֿונען אַ פֿאַרטל װי
אַזױ איבערצורײַסן בײַ דער הדסן די בתולים. אין איר גאַנצקייט האָט הדס נישט געװוּסט
אַז עפּעס איז דאָ נישט װי ס'באַדאַרף צו זײַן. זי האָט שױן ליב געהאַט דעם אַנשל מיט
אַ גרױסער ליבשאַפֿט. לױט דעם דין מוזן זיך חתן-כּלה אָפּשײדן אױף זיבן טעג נאָך
דער ערשטער באַהאָפֿטונג. צו מאָרגנס האָבן אַנשל און אַבֿיגדור אָנגעהױבן לערנען
צוזאַמען מסכת נידה. װען די קלױז האָט זיך אױסגעלײדיקט און בײַדע יונגע לײט זענען
געבליבן אַלײן, האָט אַבֿיגדור קלינגעריש און שעמעװודיק <u>אַ פֿרעג געטאָן אַנשלען װי</u>
<u>ס'איז אים צוגעגאַנגען די נאַכט</u> מיט הדסן און אַנשל האָט אָנגעזעטיקט זײַן נײַגער און
זיך געשושקעט מיט אים ביז פֿאַר נאַכט.[52]

In both the Yiddish and the English, the pronoun "he" is maintained in referring to Anshel, but only because the perspective is Avigdor's, who still believes that Anshel/Yentl is a man. Interpretation, we are reminded, depends on the beholder, who can be deceived or just plain wrong. The scene of deception is much more sexually explicit in the story than in the movie, and even more so in the Yiddish than in the English. It is not merely, as the English has it, that the marriage is consummated and Hadass is "deflowered." The Yiddish words "*bahoftn*" and especially "*ibertsuraysn*" are at once more graphic and more violent. In the Yiddish, the in-laws enter the bridal chamber to see if the man has joined with or copulated with the woman; Hadass's virginity is described as ripped, or torn.

What is the effect of these changes? With each distancing from Bashevis's text—from Yiddish to English and then from text to screen—we witness an increasing anxiety about transgression, an increasing unwillingness to defy the supposed norms of the community. Bashevis's urge to test the limits emerges from the early twentieth-century Eastern European world where the boundaries between male and female, Jew and non-Jew, here and there, are clearer than they were soon to become and were often considered too confining. For Bashevis, in Yiddish, allowing Yentl to cross over into Anshel means allowing her to choose her own way, to be free of the identity imposed upon her from without. And freedom for Yentl means freedom within Judaism. There are precedents for women studying Torah; they are limited and controversial, and these women are exceptional, but they do exist.[53] According to Jewish law, Yentl should not dress as a man; she should certainly not marry a woman. But who in the modern Jewish world can fault her for wanting to learn? In typical form, Bashevis affirms both the desire to study and to be a Jew in all senses of the word *and* the desire to break free of the strictures of the law and its customs. Near the end of the story, Anshel reveals himself to Avigdor. He undresses to prove that he is a woman. Anshel refuses to marry the man she/he has loved because she/he will not be constrained by the drudgery that would replace the life of study they have shared. Anshel's disappearance leaves Avigdor and Hadass free to marry each other, but, more significantly, it leaves Yentl free to continue to live as Anshel.

The situation is strikingly different for the English reader and viewer, beset less by the urge to test the limits of identity than by the need to define and maintain a community—a community of readers, of Jews, of men and women—which seems to be at its end. The problem for the Yiddish reader is that believing that this scenario can take place—that Yentl can become a man in order to study, and then manage to pass as one—requires an enormous leap of faith, a suspension of disbelief that Bashevis wants to insist on but which is clearly a literary construct. For the English reader it seems all too plausible, as gender barriers and the identity of the Jew in America and the modern world bear less and less resemblance to what they had once more clearly been. In English, allowing Yentl to cross over into any number of other identities is too plausible and thus too threatening. In the middle of the twentieth century, in the wake of the Holocaust, even in the wake of assimilation, this crossing over seemed both possible and perilous. One way a community defines itself is by keeping distinctions clear, by highlighting its differences from others. The fears of intermarriage, of miscegenation, of gay marriage, are all current and dramatic illustrations of a similar anxiety about group identities. The assertion of clear distinctions becomes an obvious, comforting way of maintaining the differences between groups. Who is in and who is out of the group matters most when groups are insecure about their own identities.

The transgression that is translation—the carrying over from one place to another—turns out to be not so transgressive after all, or at least transgressive in a surprising way. In translations from Bashevis's Yiddish into Singer's English we repeatedly encounter an urge to soften, to critique, but respectfully, to honor the dead and the mute. When Streisand carried over the story of Yentl into an American musical film, she certainly muted the bolder transgressions of the Yiddish, but she only carried further the tendencies to do what was already displayed in the English text. We have seen a similar pattern throughout Singer's work. It will perhaps strike contemporary readers as ironic that, in each case, it is the Yiddish text that is more radical, more willing to explore the various possibilities of identity, more assertive of the individual, more prepared to revolt. English has its eye on a different consumer in a different milieu. This observation is neither a disparagement of the English nor a plea for the Yiddish. It is, rather, simply an acknowledgment of the different readership, context, and time each version addresses.

CHAPTER 4

Returning to and from the Ghetto

YANKEV GLATSHTEYN

A "trot" is like a pair of spectacles for the weak-sighted: a translation is like a book in Braille for the blind.

—W. H. Auden

W E have seen how the act of translation can be understood as betrayal, as transgression, and as rescue. The Italian adage "*traduttore, traditore*" (translator, traitor) has been amply illustrated and not only in the case of Yiddish. Translation, in this view, is a kind of lie in which violence is done to one language—to its culturally specific cadences and resonances—so that those who live in another language may find it less foreign. Translation compels a text to assume a new identity and then presents it to a different audience as though no significant transformation had actually taken place. How, readers must ask, is the original text thus betrayed? Or is it a new audience that is betrayed, duped into accepting the illusion of sameness between an inaccessible source and a version of that source in their own language? Conventional wisdom acknowledges that "something is lost in the translation." I want to continue exploring, through close readings, the assertion that what is gained may be ultimately far more impressive.

For decades, I have found myself returning to a poem I reread often, that I have taught repeatedly, and about which I have already written at some length.[1] But this time, in addition to returning to the close reading I offered in my earlier work, I would like to consider the poem as it has been interpreted and given new life by its translators. In April 1938, Yankev Glatshteyn published his famous and controversial poem "A gute nakht, velt" ("Good Night, World").[2] In the following decades, translators repeatedly turned to it. When he wrote the poem, Glatshteyn was one of the leading modernists in American Yiddish letters. He was a leader of the *inzikhistn*—the introspectivists—who had proclaimed a new poetic day in Yiddish, one in which free rhyme and rhythm were to be expected, in which the poet's primary responsibility was to give expression to his own psyche.

All that changed dramatically when Glatshteyn wrote this poem. "Good Night, World" asks whether it is still possible for Jews to live in a post-Enlightenment world that had once granted them at least the promise of citizenship. It seems to bid farewell to that world, claiming a return to the familiar, limited environment of the Jewish ghetto. Or does it? Amid a yearning for this seemingly perfect (and perhaps nonexistent) place, this poem also, as I have argued, reveals the ambivalence of Glatshteyn's return, indeed the impossibility of such a return, the impossibility of giving up on modernity or literary modernism. Ultimately, the poem struggles with the question of where to turn now, in 1938, in a world where violent anti-Semitism is the law of some lands and much worse is threatened.

Glatshteyn recorded his own reading of the poem.[3] In his deep voice, with its Lublin Polish-Yiddish accent, Glatshteyn lets us hear the increasingly ominous movement of his poem, its attempt—necessarily unsuccessful—at restraint. He doesn't so much declaim the poem, as proclaim it. He reads it as though it were a proclamation: crisp, declarative, defiant. Only in the poem's last lines does the voice soften as if to embrace the Jewish world to which he is returning; at the end, the barely suppressed anger that he has not been able or willing to conceal is replaced by the sound of a man in mourning, a man going home to mourn.

א גוטע נאַכט, וועלט

א גוטע נאַכט, וועלט.
גרויסע, שטינקנדיקע וועלט.
נישט דו, נאָר איך פֿאַרהאַק דעם טויער.
מיט דעם לאַנגן כאַלאַט,
מיט דער פֿײַערדיקער, געלער לאַט,
מיט דעם שטאָלצן טראָט,
אויף מײַן אייגענעם געבאָט —

גיי איך צוריק אין געטאָ.

וויש אָפ, צעטרעט אַלע געשאַמדטע שפּורן.

כ'וואַלגער זיך אין דײַן מיסט,

לויב, לויב, לויב,

צעהויקערט אידיש לעבן.

קײַרעם, וועלט, אויף דײַנע טרײַפֿענע קולטורן.

כאַטש אַלץ איז פֿאַרוויסט,

שטויב איך זיך אין דײַן שטויב,

טרויעריק אידיש לעבן.

כאַזערישער דאַטש, איפֿעשדיקער ליאַך,

אַמאָלעק גאָנעוו, לאַנד פֿון זײפֿן און פֿרעסן.

שלאָברע דעמאָקראַטיע, מיט דײַנע קאַלטע

סימפּאַטיע-קאָמפּרעסן.

אַ גוטע נאַכט, עלעקטעריש צעכוצפֿעטע וועלט.

צוריק צו מײַן קעראָסין, כײלעוונעם שאָטן,

אייביקן אָקטאָבער, דריבנע שטערן,

צו מײַנע קרומע גאַסן, הויקערדיקן לאַמטערן,

מײַנע שיימעס, מײַן סווואַרבע,

מײַנע גמאָרעס, צו די האַרבע

סוגיעס, צום ליכטיקן איווורעטײַטש,

צום דין, צום טיפֿן מײן, צום כויוו, צום גערעכט.

וועלט, איך שפּאַן מיט פֿרייד צום שטילן געטאָ-לעכט.

אַ גוטע נאַכט. כ'גיב דיר, וועלט, צושטײַער

אַלע מײַנע באַפֿרײַער.

נעם צו די יעזוסמאַרקסעס, ווערג זיך מיט זייער מוט.

קראַפּיר איבער אַ טראָפּן פֿון אונדזער געטויפֿט בלוט.

און איך האָב האָפֿן אַז כאַטש ער זאַמט זיך,

גייט אויף טאָג-איין-טאָג-אויס מײַן וואַרטן.

ס'וועלן נאָך רוישן גרינע בלעטער

אויף אונדזער בוים דעם פֿאַרקוואָרטן.

איך דאַרף קיין טרייסט נישט.

איך גיי צוריק צו דאַלעד אַמעס,

פֿון וואַגנערס געץ-מוזיק צו ניגון, ברומען.

כ'קוש דיך, פֿאַרקאַלטנט אידיש לעבן.

ס'וויינט אין מיר די פֿרייד פֿון קומען.[4]

For reasons that will become clear in the following analysis, I believe the translation by the Harshavs is closest to the poetic tone and ambivalent embrace of the ghetto that is found in Glatshteyn's Yiddish. (Full disclosure: I worked on the anthology in which this version appeared, comparing the Harshavs' translations back against the original Yiddish poems, and my partiality to it no doubt stems from the sense of discovery and poetic and scholarly excitement of that work.)

"GOOD NIGHT, WORLD," TRANSLATED BY BENJAMIN AND BARBARA HARSHAV

Good night, wide world.
Big, stinking world.
Not you, but I, slam the gate.
In my long robe,
With my flaming, yellow patch,
With my proud gait,
At my own command—
I return to the ghetto.
Wipe out, stamp out all the alien traces.
I grovel in your dirt,
Hail, hail, hail,
Humpbacked Jewish life.
A ban, world, on your unclean cultures.
Though all is desolate,
I roll in your dust,
Gloomy Jewish life.

Piggish German, hostile Polack,
Sly Amalek, land of guzzling and gorging.
Flabby democracy, with your cold
Compresses of sympathy.
Good night, world of electrical insolence.
Back to my kerosene, tallowy shadow,
Eternal October, wee little stars,
To my crooked alleys, hunchbacked street-lamp,
My stray pages, my Twenty-Four-Books,
My Talmud, to the puzzling

Questions, to the bright Hebrew-Yiddish,
To Law, to deep meaning, to duty, to right.
World, I stride with joy to the quiet ghetto-light.

Good night. I grant you, world,
All my liberators.
Take the Jesusmarxes, choke on their courage.
Drop dead on a drop of our baptized blood.
And I believe that even though he tarries,
Day after day rises my waiting.
Surely, green leaves will rustle
On our withered tree.
I do not need consolation.
I go back to my four walls,
From Wagner's pagan music—to tune, to humming.
I kiss you, tangled Jewish life.
It cries in me, the joy of coming.

April 1938[5]

Within months of its publication, "A gute nakht, velt" had been translated and published in English. In the following decades it would be translated again and again, an unusual phenomenon for any Yiddish text and a clear sign of how deeply the poem continues to resonate. The following analysis considers nine of those translations, spanning seven decades, the first published within months of the Yiddish poem and the most recent in a medium Glatshteyn would never have imagined: an online blog. They are by a range of translators, poets, and interested readers. And there is a revealing gap in the dates at which translations appeared. Joseph Leftwich's 1939 translation stood alone for almost thirty years, as if in eloquent testimony to the solitary mourning of the times. It is, as well, a testimony to the status of Yiddish translation in the decades following World War II. Although Leftwich's poem reappeared several times (in 1944 in London and in 1957 and 1961 in New York), no new translation of the poem was published until Moshe Spiegel's in 1967. Spiegel was a well-known translator of Russian and Yiddish, but his version of the poem, printed in the *Chicago Jewish Forum*, is dependent on Leftwich; it was not widely read and has not been reprinted (and, as will be clear below, for good reason). It was followed in quick succession by the more often-cited versions by Ruth Whitman in 1968, Marie Syrkin in 1969, and Etta Blum in 1970.[6] As if to illustrate the low regard in which translation was then held, there is another publication of "Good Night, World" that bears no translator's name. After Glatshteyn's death in 1971, *World Jewry*, a London-based magazine published by the World Jewish Congress (with which Glatshteyn had been connected as editor of its Yiddish publication, *Folk un velt* [People and World]) printed "Good Night, World," along with his poem "Without Jews." Without other attribution—even the language of composition is omitted, though Glatshteyn is identified as "one of the finest Yiddish poets of our generation"—the English poem appears as though penned by Glatshteyn himself. In fact, it is Etta Blum's translation, with some minimal differences.[7] Then there is another chronological break until Benjamin and Barbara Harshavs' translation in 1986, Richard Fein's in 1987, Barnett Zumoff's in 1993, and Zackary Sholem Berger's in 2004.[8] These translations are beautiful, and inevitably flawed, and, most of all, they are astoundingly revealing documents. Examining the choices each of the translators made seems like an archeological expedition, unearthing and exploring clues to the shifting sands of Yiddish culture in America. Indeed, these poems offer us a history in miniature of this culture—its reception, its popularity, the mythic burdens of memory keeping it was compelled to assume, its shifting reputation as an authentic carrier of Jewish culture.

In the early years of the poem's new life in English, it was interpreted as a battle cry urging a return to the boundaries of tradition. Thus, when Joseph Leftwich published the poem's first translation in his anthology of Yiddish poetry, *The Golden Peacock* (1939), he went so far as to change its title. Leftwich renamed it "Back to the Ghetto," and from the title on, he firmly fixed for the English reader this controversial "message" of the poem. In 1939, as in 1938, the call to return to the ghetto could still be understood as a dramatic poetic image. We must remember that Glatshteyn was referring not to the Nazi ghettos, which he could not yet have imagined in 1938, but rather to the medieval Italian ghetto or to the metaphoric ghetto of London's East End or New York's Lower East Side. Repeatedly, Leftwich added words and whole phrases to underscore the finality of this return. He offered a rhyme scheme meant to echo Glatshteyn's own, but modern Yiddish poetry has a greater tolerance for rhyme than English has, and Leftwich's rhymes are far more numerous and regular than Glatshteyn's are. Leftwich also reduced Glatshteyn's forty-two-line poem to twenty-nine lines, omitting the second stanza entirely for reasons about which we can only speculate. Perhaps those lines named too many of the enemies of the Jews to be quite seemly; perhaps the references to the

twenty-four books (of the Hebrew Bible) and to the Talmud and Jewish herme-
neutics seemed too particularly Jewish and incomprehensible to the English
reader; perhaps the poem struck him as too long; perhaps the tension between
these enemies and these Jewish sites was too great to admit, much less resolve.
Whatever may have motivated Leftwich apparently appealed to Moshe Spiegel as well. Almost thirty years later, Spiegel called the poem "Return to the
Ghetto," making it one long stanza of thirty-three lines and still refraining
from naming the enemies Glatshteyn had brazenly cursed in his poem.

When Ruth Whitman first translated "Good Night, World" in 1968, she
restored the original title and, with it, more of the interpretive possibilities
of Glatshteyn's Yiddish poem. Subsequent translators have followed suit.
Though Whitman's poem seems rather daring when compared to the two
that preceded it, it has, in the natural course of translated things, been
eclipsed by these subsequent versions—written for a very different Jewish and
non-Jewish audience—that have strived even further toward unearthing
Glatshteyn's complex meanings.[9] The English-reading world is better off for
these more recent efforts, because the force of the poem, its grave and uncertain sense of importance, comes precisely from the ambiguities of its speaker.

"Good Night, World," we can accurately say, is a poem that is built on its
own tensions. Translators from Whitman forth would try to resolve these in
varying ways. Glatshteyn's farewell to the world may be defiant, but it is also
bitter and defensive. The speaker hates the world that he rejects and hurls
insults at it, but he also cannot leave it alone. "Not you, but I slam the gate"
is, at best, a disingenuous claim since Glatshteyn and his readers know full
well that the speaker has no real choice in this gesture. It is made in anticipation of an imminent catastrophe and not, as the poet claims, proudly, at his
own command, and certainly not of his own free will.

It is worth pausing over the opening lines of each English version of the
poem, in chronological order. Glatshteyn's opening lines: *A gute nakht, velt.
/ Groyse, shtinkndike velt. / Nisht du, nor ikh farhak dem toyer. / Mit dem langn
khalat, / mit der fayerdiker, geler, lat, / mit dem shtoltsn trot, / af mayn eygenem
gebot / gay ikh tsurik in geto.*

1. JOSEPH LEFTWICH, "BACK TO THE GHETTO," 1939

Good night, big world,
Great big stinking world.
Not you, but I bang the door and break off the latch.

With a long gabardine,
With a flaming yellow patch,
With proud step <u>and mien</u>,
At my own command I go
Back to the ghetto.

2. MOSHE SPIEGEL, "RETURN TO THE GHETTO," 1967

<u>Back to the crooked alleys and the flickering lamp wicks</u>—
Good night, great world,
Huge, reeking world.
It is not you but I
Who slam the gate!
In pride <u>and of my own free will</u>,
In my long gabardine with its blazing yellow badge,
I go back to the ghetto.

3. RUTH WHITMAN, 1968

Good night, wide world,
big stinking world.
Not you but I slam shut the gate.
With a long gabardine,
with a fiery yellow patch,
with a proud stride,
<u>because I want to</u>,
I'm going back to the ghetto.

4. MARIE SYRKIN, "GOOD NIGHT, WIDE WORLD," 1969

Good night, wide world
Big stinking world!
Not you but I slam shut the door.
With my long gabardine,
My fiery, yellow patch,
With <u>head erect</u>,
And at <u>my sole</u> command,
I go back into the ghetto.

5. ETTA BLUM, 1970

Good night, vast world,
big stinking world!
It's not you, but I, who slam the door.
Stepping proudly in my long cloak
with its blazing yellow patch,
I return to the ghetto
of my own free will.

In each case, the underlined words indicate the translator's interpretive choice or emphatic words he or she has added to Glatshteyn's poem. Where Glatshteyn says he bids farewell to the "big, stinking world" (line 2), Leftwich has a "great big stinking world"; presumably driven by the need for rhyme, his poem's speaker not only bangs the door but breaks off the latch (to follow "patch"); not only his step but his entire demeanor ("mien" to rhyme with "gabardine") is proud. Spiegel introduces free will into the discussion—a trope Blum echoes—as a translation of *mayn eygenem gebot* / "my own command." Free will raises the stakes in the question of individual agency. The Yiddish poem's speaker commands himself to return to the ghetto; this English poem's speaker goes further, invoking a term that insists on his ability to make rational, moral decisions even when freedom of action is limited. Spiegel first changes the order of the Yiddish lines to give pride of place to the crooked alleys and flickering lamp wicks of the Jewish ghetto to which the speaker returns. Whitman offers a less politically and philosophically resonant (and problematic) concept than free will, translating Glatshteyn's "at my own command" as a simple "because I want to." Syrkin, who emphasizes the breadth of the world in her title (adding "wide") renders this line as "at my sole command," underscoring the loneliness both of this act of return and of the individual who is compelled to make it.

Compare those lines with the more direct, less augmented versions of the later translations.

6. BENJAMIN AND BARBARA HARSHAV, "GOOD NIGHT, WORLD," 1986

Good night, wide world.
Big, stinking world.
Not you, but I, slam the gate.

In my long robe,
With my flaming, yellow patch,
With my proud gait,
At my own command—
I return to the ghetto.

7. RICHARD FEIN, 1987

Good night, wide world,
great, stinking world.
Not you, but I slam the gate.
With the long gabardine,
with the yellow patch—burning—
with proud stride
I decide-:
I am going back to the ghetto.

8. BARNETT ZUMOFF, 1993

Good night, wide world,
Great stinking world;
Not you but I slam the gate.
With my long black coat
And my fiery yellow patch,
With a proud step
And at my own command,
I go back to the ghetto.

9. ZACKARY SHOLEM BERGER, 2004 (IN *LYRIC* AND ONLINE)

Good night, world,
big stinking world.
Not you, but I slam the door.
With my long robe,
fiery yellow patch
and proud step,
at my own command
I'm going back into the ghetto.

Even if we acknowledge—as we should and must—the individual taste and poetic sensibilities of these translators, the differences between the earlier and later groupings of translations are striking. A pattern begins to emerge. Each of these later versions is at some pains to maintain the declarative sentences and crisp, almost staccato, rhythm of the Yiddish poem's opening. With the exception of Fein, each of these translators understands that troublesome line "*af mayn eygenem gebot*" as "at my own command." "Order" might have been another literal rendition of "*gebot*," but that would have erased the religious echoes of a commandment given and received. The awkward punctuation of Fein's "I decide-:" is perhaps testament to the way this line needs to be set off, contemplated, reinterpreted.

We seem to be observing an aesthetic and cultural turn in translation studies and in American Jewish culture. With the more recent versions of the poem in mind, the early translations of "Good Night, World" are even more remarkable. These earlier translators, it seems, feel constrained by their need for clarity; they are uncertain in the face of the poem's uncertainty, and they cannot afford the ambiguity that animates Glatshteyn's poem. The earliest translations of the poem are at greater pains to diminish the tensions in it, to emphasize the proud and unequivocal nature of the speaker's return.

The differences between these groups of translations illuminate two major shifts that occurred in the 1970s and that have been invoked in chapter 1. One emerges from the state of translation theory of the pre- and post-1970s, and the other from the state of Jewish American culture in the same period.

Consider Walter Benjamin's "The Task of the Translator" (in English in 1968) and George Steiner's *After Babel* (1975).[10] In one of the wonderfully serendipitous instances that scholarship sometimes provides, there is an extraordinary link between Glatshteyn's poem and these foundational theorists. Benjamin's essay first appeared in English in *Delos* in the same issue where Ruth Whitman's first published translation of "Good Night, World" also appeared. Hers is a pivotal work not only because it restored Glatshteyn's title but also because of the publication in which it was found. *Delos* published translations with the facing original, and so Benjamin's German can be found opposite the English provided by James Hynd and E. M. Valk, and Glatshteyn's Yiddish can be found some forty pages later, opposite Whitman's English.[11] And to strengthen the connections, it is also worth noting that George Steiner joined the editorial board of *Delos* with its second issue, the issue in which Benjamin's essay and Glatshteyn's poem appeared. This issue of *Delos* also published a symposium titled "The State of Translation," with more than two dozen comments by critical luminaries including W. H. Auden, William Burroughs, Northrop Frye, Michael Hamburger, Frank Kermode, Robert Lowell, and Lionel Trilling. This is all more than coincidence. It is a pattern suggesting that this is a pivotal period in translation studies, one in which we witness a remarkable burgeoning of poetic, critical, and theoretical interest in translation. Bound in the same covers, the fortunes of Glatshteyn in translation are materially linked to the fortunes of translation itself.

In addition to the increased interest in translation, as we have seen in the previous chapter, the 1970s are also the years during which Isaac Bashevis Singer's reputation (also always in translation) soared and, with it, came a noticeable rise in the market for translations from Yiddish into English and other languages. In the case of Yiddish, as it became more distanced and threatened, its translators tended to become more faithful.

At the same time, these years saw the increasing assertiveness of Jewish culture in America. This growth of a new American Judaism can be traced to Jewish responses to the Arab-Israeli wars of 1967 (and, to a lesser extent, 1973) and to the U.S. "roots" and Black Power movements of the 1970s. A proliferation of courses about the Holocaust was seen at universities around the country and a more general popular culture interest in the Holocaust also grew enormously during the 1970s. The study of Yiddish, and Americans' interest in heritage languages in general, was also on the rise. The sociolinguist Joshua Fishman has documented just how widespread this growing focus on Americans' mother tongues was. In the 1940 U.S. census, nearly 1.8 million people claimed Yiddish as their native language. Between 1940 and 1960, the U.S. Census Bureau reported an entirely predictable 45 percent decrease in this number. But then, between 1960 and 1970, there was a 66 percent *increase* in those claiming Yiddish as their mother tongue. Although this number declined by 1980, the 1980 figure was still 42 percent higher than that of 1960, with 1.2 million people still claiming Yiddish as the language of their childhood homes, nearly half a million more than in 1960.[12] (The 1990 census showed a similar decline, but the number was still higher than that found in 1960.) These statistics defy logic, history, and demographics. Certainly, neither birthrates nor immigration can account for these numbers. What they attest to, however, is a new and growing willingness, even great eagerness, to claim a different language and with it a distinct ethnic identity. Fishman found a similar trajectory for other language and ethnic groups—Chinese,

Korean, Dutch, German, and Italian—in the United States during these decades. By the end of the 1960s, this country was awash in models for reclaiming an ethnic or racial heritage, and with these came a model for Jewish assertiveness and distinctiveness as well. American Jews were willing to embrace Yiddish both because of the dynamics within the Jewish community and as a response to the culture surrounding them.

In the translations of "Good Night, World" in the pre- and post-1970s, we can clearly discern the effects of these changing times. The translations of Glatshteyn's poem between the 1930s and 1970s addressed a beleaguered Jewish world, a world still in mourning. The translations of the 1980s and beyond addressed a remarkably more confident Jewish culture. Not only did they appear amid a new interest in Yiddish literature and other identifiably Jewish markers—not least of them the Holocaust itself—but their readership could also be expected to extend beyond the Jewish community. If they appear rather less belligerent than the earlier translations, it is undoubtedly because they emerge from a different aesthetic and political sensibility. Like Glatshteyn's own poem, they are both less apologetic and less polemical than their predecessors.

We can see these differences in tone by exploring Glatshteyn's description of transition from one world to another—one irreconcilably different—and back again. His language reveals the anguish that these movements caused him; the varied language used by his translators seems to reveal both the poem's torments and the torment of the act of translation itself. In his first stanza, as we have seen, Glatshteyn renders the world as wide, large, and stinking; he asserts—though unconvincingly—that he and not the world is slamming shut the gate and that he wears the traditional garb of the Jew back to the ghetto. He hurls adjectives at the wide world that derive from Hebrew and that resound with the language of religious particularism—"geshmadte shpurn" (traces of conversion), "treyfene kulturn" (nonkosher cultures)—and he condemns it with "kheyrem" (excommunication). These are curses, words that proscribe all that is forbidden and that place the object of these curses beyond the bounds of Jewish law or life. Translations of these lines vary remarkably; once again, their differences are telling.

Glatshteyn: *Vish op, tsetret ale geshmadte shpurn.* / . . . / *kheyrem velt af dayne treyfene kulturn.*

Leftwich (1939): All apostate traces I stamp out, obliterate, / ... / I bar your unclean cultures, world, I erect against them a wall.

Spiegel (1967): I tread down all apostate traces.

Whitman (1968): Wipe away, stamp out every vestige of conversion. / ... / Damn your soiled culture, world. [Whitman's later version has "dirty culture."]

Syrkin (1969): Wipe off all markings of apostasy! / ... / I cast out all your unclean cultures, world!

Blum (1970): Erase, / stamp out all traces of apostasy! / ... / Anathema, world, on your defiled civilization!

Harshavs (1986): Wipe out, stamp out all the alien traces. / ... / A ban, world, on your unclean cultures.

Fein (1987): Wipe out, stamp out all traces of apostasy. / ... / Go to hell, with your polluted cultures, world.

Zumoff (1993): Erase and stamp out all traces of assimilation— / ... / Anathema, world upon your unclean cultures.

Berger (2004): Trampling baptismal traces. / ... / To hell, world, with your polluted cultures.

Characteristically, Leftwich adds to an already dramatic renunciation and makes the speaker more active, not only barring the world, but also erecting a (ghetto?) wall. Spiegel doesn't confront the complications of "*treyfene*" and "*kheyrem*." Whitman calls "*geshmadte*" by its proper name, invoking "conversion" at the same historical moment that it was becoming an increasingly fraught issue of concern in the American Jewish community. Blum renders "*treyfene kulturn*" as "defiled civilization," adding an exclamation point for emphasis. The Harshavs and Zumoff, like Leftwich and Syrkin before them, understand "*treyfene*" as "unclean," thus diminishing the religious resonance of *treyf*, but clarifying the meaning for the English reader. Several translators have interpreted "*geshmadte shpurn*" as "apostasy" (Leftwich, Spiegel, Syrkin, Blum, and Fein), but the Harshavs once again remove the religious invocations by rendering it as "alien," while Zumoff adds the interpretive sociological sting of "assimilation." Fein moves even further from the language of religious practice, translating the line as "Go to hell, with your polluted cultures, world," a damnation Berger echoes. At the same time, Berger gives us the baptismal fount as the locus of the "polluted cultures" of the world. These variations are dramatic illustrations of the problem of translating religious and culturally resonant Jewish concepts for a wider audience.

The images Glatshteyn uses to embrace the Jewish world are far from attractive: they are steeped in filth and dust, hunchbacked, crooked, withered, tangled. The transitional lines "*kh'valger zikh in dayn mist, / loyb, loyb, loyb, / tsehoykert yidish lebn*" (I wallow in your garbage, / Praise, praise, praise, / Hunchbacked Jewish life) encapsulate Glathstyen's ambivalence in another way. (These lines are to be found in the ellipses above.) Translators have puzzled over these lines, which ultimately hinge on a comma. Here, the punctuation determines what we understand by the possessive "your" in the line "I wallow in your garbage"; the punctuation also helps us understand just what is being praised (or at least makes us better guessers).

LEFTWICH (1939):

> In your dust and mire I sprawl,
> Praise, praise, praise,
> Crippled Jewish life.

SPIEGEL (1967):

> I bathe in your dust,
> O maimed Jewish life.

WHITMAN (1968):

> I roll around in your refuse—
> Praise, praise, praise—
> hunchbacked Jewish life.

WHITMAN (1972):

> *I roll around in your garbage*—
> praise, praise, praise—
> hunchbacked Jewish life.

SYRKIN (1969):

> I roll my body in your grime;
> Glory, glory, glory to you,
> Crippled Jewish life!

BLUM (1970):

> Praise, praise, praise,
> Humpbacked Jewish existence!
> I wallow in your filth.

HARSHAVS (1986):

> I grovel in your dirt,
> Hail, hail, hail,
> Humpbacked Jewish life.

FEIN (1987):

> I wallow in your filth.
> Blessed, blessed, blessed,
> hunchbacked Jewish life.

ZUMOFF (1993):

> I am wallowing in your garbage.
> Praise, praise, praise
> O crippled Jewish life.

BERGER (2004):

> I roll in your garbage.
> Praise to you, praise, praise,
> hunchbacked Jewish life.

Following upon the desire to wipe away all traces of conversion, to what does "*dayn mist*" (your garbage) refer? In whose garbage does the speaker now wallow, the garbage of the corrupted world being left or that of the Jewish world to which the speaker goes? If the latter, then the grammar and the gist of this sentence suggest that the speaker is trying—desperately, not altogether successfully—to praise a deformed and dirty Jewish life. A period after the first line would imply that he is wallowing in the garbage he seeks to leave in leaving the wider world he has just been cursing. But a comma inextricably links garbage, praise, and the hunchbacked Jewish life to which he now turns. As printed on the first page of the journal *Inzikh* (1938), again in Glatshteyn's volume of poetry, *Gedenklider* (1943), and yet again as the first poem of the volume *Kh'tu dermonen* (1967), these three lines indeed form one sentence, with a period ending them and commas separating the first two.[13] They compel us to read them again because—no matter how much poetic license we allow—they defy simple understanding. The interjected praise, "*loyb, loyb, loyb*," is an unmistakable echo of the liturgical "*kadosh, kadosh, kadosh*"— "holy, holy, holy"—repeated morning, noon, and night as an affirmation of faith.[14] But, in this context, his praise is ironic at best. Rhyme links "*loyb*" to "*shtoyb*" (dust) as clearly as proximity and punctuation link it to "*mist*" (garbage). Instead of God and a declaration of holiness, we have dust and garbage. In the absence of any meaningful action the speaker can take, the very dust now embraced is both verb and noun. "*Shtoyb ikh zikh in dayn shtoyb*"—literally "I en-dust myself in your dust." The gate-slamming of the third line, the destructive actions heaped upon the world, has become a reflexive construction ("*ikh shtoyb zikh*"), an action that cannot quite be imagined.

Only two of the translations—by Leftwich and the Harshavs (another instance of commonality between the first translation and one of the later ones)—punctuate these lines as Glatshteyn himself did, with a comma linking the praise and the dust. (Leftwich adds "mire" to the "dust," for reasons that remain unclear.) Spiegel omits the problematic praise entirely. Whitman ends her "I roll around in your refuse" (in 1972 the refuse becomes "garbage") with an enigmatic dash before the "praise" that follows. (In her 1972 book, *The Selected Poems of Jacob Glatstein*, these lines are also italicized, as if to set them off even more.) Syrkin separates "grime" from "glory" with a semicolon, a sign of equivocation just between joining the two thoughts and separating them completely. Blum avoids the problem altogether by changing the order of lines. As a result, there is no doubt that "humpbacked Jewish existence" (liberally punctuated by an exclamation point) is what should be the object of praise. Fein, Zumoff, and Berger choose to end the first line with a period, as if hoping to assert a kind of grammatical order over this unruly sentiment.

From here we move to the second stanza, in which the poem suggests—but does not make utterly explicit—a rejection of the enemies of the Jews: "*Khaz-erisher datsh, ipeshdiker lyakh, | Amalek ganef, land fun zoyfn un fresn. | Shlabre demokratye, mit dayne kalte | simpatye-kompresn* (Piggish German, hostile Polack, / Sly Amalek, land of guzzling and gorging. / Flabby democracy, with your cold / Compresses of sympathy).[15] Here we have two sentences that are really fragments, naming names and even coarse activity ("guzzling" and "gorging") but lacking a verb. The speaker bids good night to all of this, now enumerated in painful and hateful detail. Yiddish readers would have needed no explanation of just who these enemies are. By 1939, in English, two of them—Germans and Poles—would have been dreadfully obvious, but the Amalekites might have needed a gloss. And, indeed, they continued to plague translators. Leftwich (1939) and Spiegel (1967), as I have indicated, refrain from naming any of them. Syrkin (1969), the Harshavs (1986), and Berger (2004) give us back "Amalek." The Harshavs add a note of explanation, describing them as "a tribe that slaughtered Jews in their exodus from Egypt and was consequently condemned by God to annihilation (Exodus 17:14). Amalek became the symbol of all the persecutors of the Jews, prefiguring the hope for their punishment."[16] Whitman (1968 and 1972), probably uncertain that her readers will understand any reference to the Amalekites, simply replaces the Amalekite thieves with a most surprising reference she hopes they will understand: thieving Rumanians! Amalek probably became Rumania through a folkloristic calque of any number of Yiddish jokes that warn people to guard their possessions and even their fingers if asked to shake hands with a Rumanian. They are the proverbial thieves of Yiddish lore. Both Blum (1970) and Zumoff (1993) echo Whitman's choice. When the periodical *World Jewry* (1971) republished Blum's translation, "Amalek" was restored to its rightful place and the Rumanians were spared further opprobrium. In this version, which does not even bear the translator's name, it is impossible to know who was responsible for the change. Fein (1987) avoids the problem of gloss by offering his own within the translation, giving us "Jew-killers" instead of naming the biblical tribe that killed the Jews on their way out of Egypt. These differences cannot simply be mapped onto a timeline. Collectively, they illustrate an uncertainty about the level of Jewish literacy among non-Yiddish readers, about what cultural or historical knowledge English readers can be assumed to know, and about how much Jewish assertiveness is acceptable.

Glatshteyn challenges his readers, translators, and critics at every turn. The poem proceeds, once again, to bid good night to the world: "*A gute nakht, elektrish tsekhutspete velt. | Tsurik tsu mayn kerosin, kheylevnem shotn*" (Good night, world of electrical insolence. / Back to my kerosene, tallowy shadow).[17] *Chutzpah* is one of those Yiddish words that pepper American speech. It means what each of the translators (except, again, for Leftwich and Spiegel, who omit it) tells us it means: "insolence" (the Harshavs—theirs is the only version to make a substantive out of Glatshteyn's adjective); "impudent" (Fein); "arrogant" (Whitman and Zumoff); "brazen" (Blum and Berger); and "brash" (Syrkin). *Chutzpah* also connotes self-assuredness, a confidence that is not entirely negative. And, indeed, though the world may be full of this *chutzpah*, it is difficult for the speaker to reject it and turn to the shadowy, crooked, hunchbacked world he now faces. Perhaps revealing the difficulty of such a turn, Glatshteyn doesn't specify *who* is to make this transition. He begins line 22 simply with "*Tsurik*" (Back). This time, the sentence has many objects, but neither verb nor subject. Glatshteyn neither names the person who is presumably going *tsurik* (back) nor tells his readers how this return is to be made. Blum is alone in adding "I," clarifying this for the reader by providing a complete sentence for Glatshteyn's incomplete thought.

And to what precisely is the speaker going back?

> *Tsurik tsu mayn kerosin, kheylevnem shotn,*
> *eybikn oktober, dribne shtern,*
> *tsu mayne krume gasn, hoykerdikn lamtern,*
> *mayne sheymes, mayn svarbe,*
> *mayne gemores, tsu di harbe*
> *sugyes, tsum likhtikn ivretaytsh,*
> *tsum din, tsum tifn meyn,*
> *tsum khoyv, tsum gerekht,*
> *velt, ikh shpan mit freyd tsum shtiln geto-lekht.*

Once again, meaning may hang on a comma. Throughout this poem, it is the *velt*/world that is being addressed and thus animated; the ghetto to which the speaker returns is object but not subject. "*Velt*" ends the line right before the lines just quoted ("*A gute nakht, elektrish tsekhutspete velt*" [Good night, world of electrical insolence]). What follows is one long list of what will be found in the Jewish ghetto, punctuated by commas. And then, grammatically and inevitably, the speaker returns to the *velt* at the end of this list: "*Velt, ikh shpan mit freyd tsum shtiln geto-lekht*" (World, I stride with joy to the quiet ghetto-light). The poem reminds us again and again that the speaker cannot simply ignore the world or turn away from it. Most of the translations follow Glatshteyn's punctuation, but Whitman and Blum do not. As we have already seen, Whitman's choice is once again the enigmatic dash, as if pointing to the "world" being left behind. The incompleteness of these lines is even more dramatically illustrated on the page by Blum's ellipsis marks. What, they seem to ask, are we missing?

SPIEGEL (1967):

> Back to my lighted kerosene and its shadows,
> Back to the crooked alleys and the flickering lamp wicks,
> Back to my Scriptures, my tractates of the Holy Law!
> With my lantern I return once more
> To the unending pilgrim search for truth and mercy.
> I retreat with deep-felt joy
> To the dim light of the ghetto.

WHITMAN (1968):

> Back to your kerosene, candle shadows,
> eternal October, minute stars,
> to my crooked streets, humped lanterns,
> my sacred pages, my Bible,
> my Gemorra, to my backbreaking
> studies, to the bright Yiddish prayerbook,
> to law, profundity, duty, justice,—
> world, I walk gladly towards quiet ghetto light.
> [Whitman's 1972 text has "tiny stars."]

SYRKIN (1969):

> Back to my kerosene, my shadowed tallow candles,
> Endless October and faint stars,
> To my twisting streets and crooked lantern,
> To my sacred scrolls and holy books,
> To tough Talmudic riddles and lucid Yiddish speech,
> To law, to duty, and to justice,
> To what is deeply mine.
> World, joyously I stride
> Toward the quiet ghetto lights.

BLUM (1970):

> I return to my kerosene and candle shadows,
> to my perpetual autumn and minute stars,
> to my crooked streets and humped lanterns.
> I return to my tattered holy pages, the Bible,
> to my Torah and the laborious learning,
> to the glowing Sacred Language;
> to the Law and the revealed exegesis,
> to duty, to integrity . . .
> With joy I pace to soft ghetto lights.

HARSHAVS (1986):

> Back to my kerosene, tallowy shadow,
> Eternal October, wee little stars,
> To my crooked alleys, hunchbacked street-lamp,
> My stray pages, my Twenty-Four-Books,
> My Talmud, to the puzzling
> Questions, to the bright Hebrew-Yiddish,
> To Law, to deep meaning, to duty, to right.
> World, I stride with joy to the quiet ghetto-light.

FEIN (1987):

> Back to my kerosene, tallowed shadows,
> eternal October, minute stars,
> to my warped streets and hunchbacked lanterns,
> my worn-out pages of the Prophets,
> my Gemaras, to arduous
> Talmudic debates, to lucent, exegetic Yiddish,
> to Rabbinical Law, to deep-deep meaning, to duty, to what is right.
> World, I walk with joy to the quiet ghetto light.

ZUMOFF (1993):

> Back to my kerosene, my tallow-candle shadows,
> Eternal October, tiny stars;
> To my crooked streets, humpbacked lanterns,

Torn old scrolls and Biblical studies,

Talmud and its difficult passages;

To glorious Yiddish,

To the sacred law, to deep meaning, to duty, to justice.

World, I stride with joy to the quiet ghetto lights.

BERGER (2004):

Back to my kerosene, candlestick shadows,

eternal October, minute stars,

to my crooked streets, hunched lanterns,

my stray pages, my twenty-four books

of Bible, my Talmud. Back to knotty

passages, to shining Yiddish glosses,

to judgment, deep intent, duty, justice:

world, I stride with joy to the quiet ghetto light.

The repetition of "to" that Syrkin and Blum give us at the beginning of several of these lines imposes another kind of poetic order and direction to the poem. This becomes not only a movement *from* but a movement *to*. But, again, we must ask, to what? The quiet ghetto light sheds light on a world that is, at first sight, shrunken, deformed, and impoverished. Again we have the *hoyker*—the hunchback—that weighs down the life of the Jew; the brightness and connections of electricity are replaced by a flickering, unsteady kerosene lamp; the stars have become petite. Then, in a more positive sense and in a quintessentially modern turn, Glatshteyn embraces the textuality of the Jews, but not their beliefs or practices. Once he has identified the literary tradition—the torn pages of holy books, the twenty-four books of the Hebrew Bible, the difficult questions that characterize the give-and-take of Talmudic debate, the Yiddish translations and explications of Hebrew texts— only then can he "walk with joy to the quiet ghetto light," embracing the law, meaning, duty, and right. But this embrace is not complete. Here, too, his choice of words is revealing. Each translator has given us "law" for Glatshteyn's "*din*," but several of them have also felt the need to qualify that translation in some way. Yiddish has no capital letters, but Blum, the Harshavs, and Fein capitalize "Law," making it clear that this is no mundane, worldly law, but a higher one; Spiegel gives us "Holy Law!" (his exclamation point). For the English reader who may still not know what Law is meant,

Fein goes further and calls it "Rabbinical Law"; Zumoff gives us "sacred law." But Glatshteyn hesitates to make precisely this connection. He does not claim to be returning to the law in the sense of *halokhe* (religious law); he thus, once again, stops just short of submitting to the religious system he invokes and that the translators reassert.

Glatshteyn also uses the breathtakingly resonant construction "*tsum tifn meyn*." This, too, has plagued translators. Whitman gives us "profundity"; Blum has the curious and rather awkward gloss of "revealed exegesis"; the Harshavs and Zumoff have "deep meaning"; Fein emphasizes the depths with "deep-deep meaning." Syrkin's variant translations are an extraordinary example of the difficulty in that "*meyn*." "*Meyn*" suggests meaning and intention; "*tifn meyn*" is "deep meaning." But *meyn* is only one little diacritical mark away from *mayn*. (We have seen the interpretive possibilities of that mark in Anna Margolin's "Maris tfile.") *Mayn* means "mine." Place a *pasekh*, or a line, under two *yuds*—the smallest letter of the Yiddish alphabet—and we move from "meaning" to "mine," from signification to possession. To confound matters even further, it is a mark that is often omitted from print, and its pronunciation depends on regional accent. And, still further, in the recording of Glatshteyn reading his own poem, you can hear him pronounce the word as *mayn*, which is entirely appropriate in his Lublin-inflected Yiddish. In two venues, Marie Syrkin has it both ways, yet another indication of the ongoing acts of interpretation we gain in multiple translations. In *A Treasury of Yiddish Poetry*, we read "what is deeply mine"; *The Literature of Destruction* gives us (as Whitman did) "profundity."[18]

So is the speaker, in fact, returning to deep meaning or to what is his? Or is the emphasis on his own sources of meaning? Here Glatshteyn exposes the other side of the tension that has marked this poem: the difficulty not of leaving the world of modernity and modernism but of claiming the Jewish world as his own. In removing the stanza, perhaps Leftwich hoped to avoid that difficulty. But unlike his earliest, and determinedly decisive, translators, Glatshteyn really does want it both ways: the wide world and the Jewish world, the worlds—both worlds—that give him deep meaning and that are his.

Glatshteyn begins the final stanza with the "good night" of his title and first line. "*A gute nakht, kh'gib dir, velt, tsushtayer, | ale mayne bafrayer. | Nem tsu di yezusmarkses, verg zikh mit zayer mut. | Krapir iber a tropn fun undzer getoyft blut*." Here the poet gives to the world all his liberators, the "jesus-marxes" on whom it is hoped the world will choke.

LEFTWICH (1939):

Good night, world, you may keep for all it matters to me,
My liberators of humanity,
My Christs and Marxes and all they would do,
Keep the baptized blood they gave to you.

SPIEGEL (1967):

Good night, world. I leave to you
Our mankind liberators;
Keep our Christs, and our Marxes,
And riot in the baptized blood of their aftermath.

WHITMAN (1968):

Good night. I'll make you, world, a gift of
all my liberators.
Take back your Jesus-Marxists, choke on their courage.
Croak over a drop of our christianized blood.

WHITMAN (1972):

Good night. I'll make you, world, a gift of
all my liberators.
Take back your Jesus-Marxes, choke on their courage.
Croak over a drop of our christianized blood.

SYRKIN (1969):

Good night, I give you in good measure
All my redeemers;
Take your Jesus Marxes; choke on their daring.
Burst with each drop of our baptized blood.

BLUM (1970):

Good night, world.
To you I donate all of my liberators.

You may keep the Jesus-Marxes
and choke on their daring!
Croak on a drop of our apostate blood!

HARSHAVS (1986):

Good night. I grant you, world,
All my liberators.
Take the Jesusmarxes, choke on their courage.
Drop dead on a drop of our baptized blood.

FEIN (1987):

Good night. It's all yours, world. I disown
my liberation.
Take back your Jesusmarxists, choke on their arrogance.
Croak on a drop of our baptized blood.

ZUMOFF (1993):

Good night. I contribute to you, O world,
All my would-be saviors.
Take the Jesus-Marxes—choke on their courage;
Devil take you for a drop of our baptized blood.

BERGER (2004):

Good night. To you, world, I donate
all my liberators.
Take the Jesusmarxes, choke on their bravery.
Die for a drop of our baptized blood.

The Yiddish "*tsushtayer*" has been translated in various ways, including
the most neutral and least assertive "keep" (Leftwich) and "leave" (Spiegel)
as well as the more literal "grant" (Harshavs), "gift" (Whitman), "contribute"
(Zumoff), and "donate" (Blum and Berger) and, more surprisingly, "disown"
(Fein). But, regardless, the contribution Glatshteyn makes to the world accen-
tuates, however ironically, that these Jesusmarxes are Jewish in origin and are

given freely. Here we have an aggressive reminder of the world's indebtedness to the Jews in whose names anti-Semitism has been most famously practiced. The difference between Whitman's first and second printing of the poem exposes another of the questions the poem continues to raise for its readers: Who is attacked in these lines? Is it the followers of Jesus and Marx (as "Jesus-Marxists" implies), or is it these figures ("Jesus-Marxes") themselves and what they taught? And, typically for Glatshteyn, the answer is both. The line takes aim at the non-Jewish world that has made these icons of Western civilization their own. It is aimed at the Jew, Marx, who famously rejected his (Jewish) origins, and at the Jew, Jesus, whose followers did the same. But it is also aimed at the Jews themselves, or at least at some Jews: those who have followed these liberators—particularly Marx—and been betrayed, and even those, like Glatshteyn himself, who sought liberation through embracing the philosophies and practices of the wider surrounding world, rejecting what they once thought of as the parochial Jewish world to which this poem seems to herald a return.

All of them are cursed with a violent end. "*Krapir iber a tropn fun undzer getoyft blut,*" Glatshteyn writes. "*Krapir*" is certainly angrier and nastier than Leftwich's "Keep the baptized blood" or Spiegel's inexplicable "riot in the baptized blood." To hear the venomous tone of this curse, we must turn to Whitman—"Croak over a drop of our christianized blood"—or to the Harshavs' "Drop dead on a drop of our baptized blood."

When "he" is invoked in the next line (line 34), Glatshteyn makes the most explicit connection to Jewish faith in the poem. "*Un ikh hob hofn az khotsh er zamt zikh*" is another grammatical construction that calls attention to itself. Instead of a straightforward *ikh hof* (I hope), Glatshteyn offers us a grammatical construction that sounds more archaic: "*ikh hob hofn*"—"I have hope," with "hope" in a rather ambiguous grammatical form: neither the common noun form, *hofnung*, nor the infinitive form, *tsu hofn*. We must wonder just what is hoped for. "He," of course, refers not to God but to the messiah, an allusion that translators have sometimes been at pains to clarify.

LEFTWICH (1939):

> I have hope though he delay
> Our redeemer will come one day.

SPIEGEL (1967):

> Though God still tarries, still I cherish the hope
> That one day He will show Himself once more.

WHITMAN (1968 AND 1972):

> For I have hope, even if He is delaying,
> day by day my expectation rises.

SYRKIN (1969):

> And still I trust that though He tarry,
> My waiting will spring newly day by day.

BLUM (1970):

> And, although He tarries,
> day and night my waiting ascends.

HARSHAVS (1986):

> And I believe that even though he tarries,
> Day after day rises my waiting.

FEIN (1987):

> And though He tarries, I have hope;
> day in, day out, my expectation grows.

ZUMOFF (1993):

> And though the Messiah tarries,
> My anticipation rises day by day.

BERGER (2004):

> I hope that though it tarries
> my waiting will rise up daily.

Only the Harshavs refrain from commenting. Leftwich makes (too) explicit the redeemer who will come; Spiegel ventures the name of God; Zumoff explains that it is the "Messiah" who tarries. Confronted again with the lack of capital letters in Yiddish, Spiegel, Whitman, Syrkin, Blum, and Fein also capitalize "He." Berger gives us "it," referring to "my waiting" and not to any imaginable redemption at all. Glatshteyn is alluding here to a passage that his Yiddish readers would have had no difficulty recognizing: Maimonides's affirmation of faith, "*Ani ma'amin*" (I believe). But Glatshteyn's use of these words is more ironic than prophetic. "*Ani ma'amin*" announces the unshakable belief in redemption, the certainty that the messiah will come. It points to his arrival.[19] "*A gute nakht, velt*" points to the process of waiting itself, rather than to a goal. Hope, not faith, and waiting, not the messiah, are the objects of Glatshteyn's imagination. It would have taken a great deal more faith than Glatshteyn had ever possessed to believe in any form of Jewish redemption in 1938.

The declaration then, in line 38, "*Ikh darf keyn treyst nisht*" (I need no consolation), is unconvincing. Consolation is precisely what he needs now. Glatshteyn announces what must be done: "*Ikh gey tsurik tsu daled ames*" (I go back to four cubits). This may be the most troublesome line of all for translators, and the one that most requires explanation. To explain what "*daled ames*" means to Jews, Leftwich gives us "my own city"; Spiegel, "my house of refuge"; Whitman, "my very beginnings"; Syrkin, "my straight and narrow way"; and Blum, "my rightful dwelling." These explain a concept that the Yiddish reader does not need to have explained. The Harshavs return us to a simpler "my four walls," echoed by Zumoff and made even more literal by Berger's "my four cubits." With the exception of Fein (who gives us the claustrophobic "our cramped space"), these varied translations return us to the pattern explored earlier: the differences among the pre- and post-1970s. Here, too, earlier translators expect less of their readers and offer stronger glosses than the later versions provide. "*Daled ames*" refers to the four cubits of space (about six feet) denoted as one's own in Talmudic discussions; it is used as a way of describing the metaphoric and literal fence that observant Jews construct around themselves and the Law. It can be used to describe a domestic space, a place of study and worship, terrain that can be marked as Jewish; it connotes a circumscribed and safe world in which rules are understood and followed, and, to be sure, it can connote a world made too small, too cramped, by those rules. Nothing in the poem has made this fence any different from the ghetto walls with which Glatshteyn began. With this reference, he celebrates a Jewishly defined universe even as he acknowledges its severely limited scope.

Though Glatshteyn turns to this space out of necessity, he refrains from claiming it as his own. The Yiddish poem has none of the possessive pronouns conspicuously added by every one of the English translations. If these are *my* or *our* four walls, it is a space the speaker occupies reluctantly. The possessive pronoun makes grammatical sense in English but is unnecessary in Yiddish. (Yiddish prefers the definite article or nothing at all: *di mame, dos kind, di heym* [the mother, child, home] is more common than *mayn mame* or *mayn kind* or *mayn heym* [my mother, child, home].) Glatshteyn's translators could have rendered this line straightforwardly as "I go back to four cubits" or "I go back to the four cubits." But the English translators choose to make of these problematic four cubits something *we* share, or something *I* reclaim.

In the absence of that possessive in the Yiddish poem, we may detect a reluctance that binds none of the English translators. Glatshteyn doesn't need the possessive, not only because it is grammatically useless, but because he need not underscore the obvious point that the *daled ames* is a familiar Jewish site and therefore part of the universe of a Yiddish poet and his readers. English translators have felt the need to make more pronounced the connection to a Jewish site that their language does not guarantee. At the same time, the absence of the possessive in the Yiddish poem is symbolically appropriate because it keeps Glatshteyn from having to limit himself to this relatively small space. In Yiddish, we are invited to ask whose four cubits these are. In English, every translator affirms that it is the speaker's or ours. In this, all the translators are consistent, despite the vast differences among them in other respects. Perhaps what we have here is an example of some of the tendencies in Jewish culture that have remained consistent since World War II: among them, the use of Yiddish as a sign of authenticity, the concern about what English readers will know and think about this culture and its speakers, the felt need to find and describe the boundaries of Jewishness.

The poem ends with Glatshteyn's beautiful, plaintive, and confusing declaration: "*S'veynt in mir di freyd fun kumen.*" The Harshavs' translation, the most literal of them all, renders this line as "It cries in me, the joy of coming." This is a convoluted construction both in Yiddish and in English. Just as earlier in the poem he refused clearly to name the point of arrival he so yearns for, Glatshteyn refrains from naming it here. Only this translation retains the open-endedness of Glatshteyn's final line. Others trace a route that leads clearly back, past Wagner, Jesus, and Marx, past electricity, democ-

Mom, this is rather boring

racy, and the possibilities of the Enlightenment and modernism, into the welcoming arms of the Jewish world. (Whitman, interestingly, had it right the first time, but returned to the difficult line to clarify it.) Tracing a route that, as I have been arguing, radically changes the tone and sense of the poem, every translator seems to long for what Glatshteyn might have longed for too, but which he did not name:

Leftwich (1939): I weep with the joy of coming back to you.

Spiegel (1967): I weep for the joy of coming back to you . . .

Whitman (1968): the joy of coming is weeping in me.

Whitman (1972): I cry with the joy of coming back.

Syrkin (1969 and 1988): The joy of homecoming weeps in me.

Blum (1970 and 1971): The joy of home-coming sobs in me.

Harshavs (1986): It cries in me, the joy of coming.

Fein (1987): Within me weeps the joy of coming home.

Zumoff (1993): The joy of coming back weeps within me.

Berger (2004): There weeps in me the joy of return.

(In case the pathos in the poem is not clear enough, Spiegel added a penultimate line—"Bending crippled under your load of sorrow"—to describe the process of the speaker's return.) Though comforting, this is a trajectory that the original poem is at some linguistic and poetic pains to counteract. It is worth noting that Glatshteyn stops short here of saying either that he is going *home* or that he is going *back*—a hesitation that almost every English translator undoes. Glatshteyn's ultimate focus was on the process of coming and not on the point of destination. He is not going back or returning to a place he ever inhabited because, as a modernist poet and a cosmopolitan modern Jew, he was never really there. (The word "*tsurik*" [back] appears in each stanza, but not in the final lines.) Yet he yearns for it. He ends with the gerund "*kumen*" (coming), as if to underscore the uncompleted nature of this movement. Even at this very end, he still cannot fully embrace the goal toward which he has been moving, stopping just short of naming the return to which he now lays claim.

Glatshteyn's poem can best be understood as a rejection of the external world that is at once genuine, deeply reflective, and transitory. In contrast, most of his translators emphasize the rejection rather than its transitory nature. These translations do not merely point to the deficiencies or insights of one translator or another—though surely some are deficient and some are better than others. Far more significant—both for our understanding of Glatshteyn's poem and for our understanding of the many manifestations of Yiddish culture—is that these translations were produced for different audiences in significantly different years, and thus the translators offer widely divergent interpretations of the original. How, indeed, could they not?

As translation theory has long promised, analyzing these different translations of Glatshteyn's poem illuminates the Yiddish poem too. Once again, we see that English translations (primarily but not exclusively) tend to mute Glatshteyn's more radical ambivalence about Jewish life and his equally radical claim that in the modern world the individual cannot be constrained by the claims of the community. What is perhaps most striking, especially in those translations produced before 1970, is how much more muted this ambivalence is, how conservative, tentative, protective, even nostalgic they sound compared to the poet's own tortured, ambivalent outcry. In this, they are rather like the American Jewish response to the Holocaust in the decades following the war: unfathomable loss triggers a nostalgic celebration of Jewish symbols, the creation of an imagined community that clings to ever-shrinking circles and that seems more willing to embrace an imaginary ghetto than their forebears ever were to embrace the real one. That nostalgia is still with us, especially in these earlier translations. Yet at the same time, later translations, addressed to a much less beleaguered community, to a community still focused on the Holocaust but at a greater remove from it, return us to the multiple turns and returns of Glatshteyn's poem. Although all share a concern with what the reader will know, what needs to be explained, and what must remain open to interpretation, later translations expect the reader to do a little more work. Glatshteyn's poem seeks to invent a modernity that translators and readers continue to imagine. He longs for a bolder and more synergistic modern world, one that includes Jewish life, however problematically figured, and also includes the wider world this poem calls into being.

CHAPTER 5

Concluding Lines
and Conclusions

R ARELY have Yiddish texts received as much or as varied attention as
Glatshteyn's poem. It is certainly noteworthy that "A gute nakht, velt"
has been translated so many times, but it is not a unique occurrence. Like the
poem, I. L. Peretz's (1852–1915) equally resonant and much-anthologized short
story "Bontshe Shvayg" has also been translated multiple times (by at least
twenty different translators).[1] The story's plot and the questions it raises are
among the most well known in Yiddish literature. A humble, abused, long-
suffering man who lived alone and in silence, Bontshe dies with no one to
mourn him. When he appears before the angels in heaven, he remains silent.
The divine court offers him a final reward: in paradise, he may ask for anything his heart desires. And then, in one of the most evocative lines in all of
Yiddish literature, Bontshe utters his only full sentence of the story. He asks
to be given a hot roll with fresh butter every morning (*"vil ikh take ale tog, in
der fri, a heyse bulke mit frisher puter"*).[2] This request is followed by the final
lines of the story, in which the silence that has permeated the story is broken
by the laughter of the prosecuting angel.

First published in Yiddish in 1894, the story's title and its final lines have
given translators pause for over a century. The following translators published the story under these titles:

Leo Wiener, "Bontsie Silent," 1899

Helena Frank, "Bontzye Shweig," 1906

Henry Goodman, "Bontche Shweig," 1947

Maurice Samuel, "Silent Bontche," 1948

Moshe Spiegel, "Buntcheh the Silent," 1958

Hilde Abel, "Bontsha the Silent," 1974

Hillel Halkin, "Bontshe Shvayg," 1990

Eli Katz, "Bontshe Shvayg," 1996[3]

In English, the "Shvayg" of the story's title is rendered as a substantive, either the character's last name or a moniker conveying his most salient feature. (Frank, indeed, underscores this by adding a footnote after the title explaining that it means "Bontzye 'mum.'") In grammatical Yiddish it can also be understood as an imperative: "Bontshe, be silent!" But this is an admonition that a reader is most likely to resist or, at the very least, to see as problematic. Why is a character—especially in a Yiddish story—told to be silent? Everything one knows about Yiddish—its orality, its history of verbose literary characters, its status as the spoken language of the Jews—seems to contradict this command. Even Jewish religious texts and practices can be marshaled to counter this command. Consider Talmudic discourse and its verbal give-and-take or the Book of Job, in which Job, unlike Bontshe, speaks at great length about his misfortunes. All this reminds us that, in Yiddish, silence is not to be considered golden and that this is more than the story of a humble, innocent man who is terribly oppressed but would be satisfied if his simple needs were satisfied. Peretz's title may be addressed to Bontshe, but we must wonder who is making this demand. And that, in turn, suggests that the title points not only to Bontshe, but also to those who would silence him. It admonishes Bontshe not to remain silent, but rather *for* remaining silent, and, most provocatively, it offers a critique of all those—Jews and anti-Semites alike—who have created the conditions that would lead a man to suffer in silence.[4]

The story's final sentence has presented an even greater interpretive challenge for translators. Peretz's story ends with

דיינים און מלאָכים האָבן אַראָפּגעלאָזט די קעפ פֿאַרשעמט; דער קטיגור האָט זיך
צעלאַכט.

[*Dayonem un malokhem hobn aropgelozt di kep farshemt; der kateyger hot zikh tselakht.*][5]

Variants in translating the final lines of "Bontshe Shvayg" include the following:

1. Judges and angels drooped their heads abashed. The Prosecuting Attorney laughed out loud. (Wiener, 353)

2. The Court and the angels looked down, a little ashamed; the prosecutor laughed. (Frank, 181)

3. The angels lower their heads in shame! The Prosecuting Attorney laughs aloud. (Goodman, 30)

4. Judges and angels looked down, ashamed. The prosecuting attorney broke into a laugh. (Samuel, 83)

5. The judges and angels were stunned. The Heavenly Informer burst into laughter. (Spiegel, 65)

6. Then the silence is shattered. The prosecutor laughs aloud, a bitter laugh. (Abel, 77)

7. The judges and angels hung their heads in shame. The prosecutor laughed. (Halkin, 152)

8. The angels and the judges lowered their heads in shame. The prosecutor burst out laughing. (Katz, 194)

The changes to Peretz's ending (here and in more than a score of other translations) were wrought by time, taste, language, and varying interpretations. Goodman's exclamation point adds emphasis where none is needed. The silence is never "shattered," as it is in Abel's sentence. *Farshemt*, as every translator knows, means "embarrassed" or "ashamed," but it is not "a *little* ashamed" (Frank), nor is it "stunned" (Spiegel). Peretz leaves open the question of whether the angels and judges are shamed by the unassuming simplicity of this man or ashamed to be implicated in a religious system that can produce such a man. The reflexive "*hot zikh tselakht*" may be more emphatic than *hot gelakht* (laughed), but it is neither "a bitter laugh" (Abel) nor quite "breaking or bursting out in laughter" (Samuel, Spiegel, and Katz). These glosses seem more critical of the laughter and thus of those who might be tempted to laugh at a man like Bontshe. Wiener's translation, appearing within five years of the story's publication, and Halkin's, appearing almost a century later, are more restrained. They return to the uncertainty of Peretz's sentence. The laughter stands alone, without comment, asking us to consider the source of the laughter, at whom it is directed, its tone, whether we are to laugh along, and whether it serves as confirmation or condemnation of Bontshe's selflessness or, rather, of his hopeless simplicity.

As with "A gute nakht, velt," it is impossible to know the extent to which earlier translations influenced later ones. We cannot trace a linear trajectory from the turn into one century, through subsequent decades, to the turn into another. All of the pre-1970s translations are unalike, as are all of the ones that appeared post-1970. But there are patterns of similarity and difference. Peretz's story poses a hermeneutic challenge that some translators are at pains to lessen. There appears, mid-twentieth century and in the shadow of the Holocaust, more of an attempt to elevate Bontshe's silence and his suffering. Peretz's anger at the passivity of Bontshe and the expectations of the world in which we find him is more muted in most of these English translations. These versions are addressed to Jews in mourning and also to other English readers, about whom we can know even less. They make a plea for understanding and sympathy. Peretz's Yiddish story is a call to arms, or at least to action. Addressed to Jews who might yet be motivated to act on their own behalf, it leaves us with the uncertainty, the accusations, and the anger that encourage response.

Leo Wiener (1862–1939), a Harvard professor of Slavic studies, offered English readers the first translation of Peretz's story and was first in other respects as well. He was appointed to Harvard's Department of Slavic Languages and Literatures in 1896 (although he never attended a university) and was promoted to assistant professor in 1901 and to full professor a decade later.[6] The first professor of Slavic studies in the United States, and one of the first Jewish professors at Harvard, Wiener was a prolific translator, primarily of Tolstoy but also of other Russian writers, as well as Czech, German, and Yiddish authors.[7] Wiener's translation of the Peretz story appeared in his *History of Yiddish Literature in the Nineteenth Century*, the first work in any language to suggest that Yiddish literature had a history worth examining and thus the first to claim a Yiddish literary canon. Wiener called the language Judeo-German. Claiming that his history was intended for "the general public and not for the linguistic scholar," he nonetheless used language that adhered to his philological interests but was unlikely to be inviting to the "general public." He appended a "Chrestomathy" section to his *History*. This literary anthology, meant to represent the best of Yiddish literature, contained translations from Yiddish opposite facing pages that were transliterated and presented "in the modified orthography of the German language."[8] Wiener's translations and transliterations may recall the efforts of Moses Mendelssohn (1729–1786), a proponent of the Haskalah (Jewish Enlightenment) who sought to bring Jews closer to the culture and language of their surroundings by undertaking the first translation of the Hebrew Bible into (High) German. Mendelssohn's translation taught German by rendering that most familiar of Jewish texts into the language of the land, a language close to the Yiddish its readers knew, and transliterating that German into Hebrew script. Wiener's chrestomathy, instead, made Yiddish accessible through its English translation and through transliteration of the Yiddish into Latin (German) script. (See below.) In addition to its anthologizing function, a chrestomathy is used by linguists to teach a language. But was it Yiddish that Wiener was teaching, or, like Mendelssohn, was he aiming at the language of the land? Mendelssohn used Hebrew script in order to teach German. It is unlikely that Wiener would have been interested in teaching English to his Yiddish readers, but he could hardly have hoped to teach Yiddish to his English readers either.

---

352   YIDDISH LITERATURE

löhnt, nor dort is' der Ōlem-hascheker, dā auf'n Ōlem-emes west du dein Lōb bekummen !

Dich wet dās Bess-din-schel-majle nischt mischpe-ten, dir wet es nischt paskenen, dir wet es kēin Cheelek nischt aus- un' nischt āb-thēilen ! Nemm dir, wās du willst ! Alles is' dein ! ‾‾‾‾

Bonzje hēbt dās erste Māl die Āugen auf ! Er werd wie verblend't vun der Licht vun alle Seiten; Alles blankt, Alles blischtschet, vun Alles jägen Strahlen : vun die Wänd', vun die Keelim, vun die Malochim, vun die Dajonim ! Ssame Sunnen !

Er läst die müde Āugen arāb.

—Take? frägt er messupek un' verschämt.

—Sicher ! entfert fest der Ow-bess-din ! Sicher, sāg' ich dir, as Alles is' dein, Alles in Himmel gehör' zu dir ! Klaub' un' nemm, wās du willst, du nemmst nor bei dir allēin !

—Take? frägt Bonzje noch a Māl, nor schōn mit a sicheren Kol.

—Take ! Take ! Take ! entfert män ihm auf sicher vun alle Seiten.

—Nu, ōb asō, schmēichelt Bonzje, will ich take alle Tāg' in der Früh' a hēisse Bulke mit frischer Putter !

Dajonim un' Malochim hāben arābgelāst die Köpp' verschämt. Der Katēgor hāt sich zulacht.

J. L. PEREZ.

Final transliterated page of Leo Wiener's "Bontsie Silent," published in *The History of Yiddish Literature in the Nineteenth Century* (Charles Scriber's Sons, 1899)

The Germanized presentation of the Yiddish made the latter more transparent, more accessible, and, perhaps most of all, more elevated than the Yiddish letters, which would have been largely incomprehensible to all but a very particular (i.e., Jewish) general reader or to a specialized scholarly reader.

Just one year before the appearance of Wiener's *History*, he published his first book that contained the first translations of Yiddish poetry into English. *Songs from the Ghetto*, published in Boston by Copeland and Day in 1898, introduced the poetry of Morris Rosenfeld to an American audience. Rosenfeld was one of the "sweatshop poets"—a group of immigrant proletarian Yiddish writers in America who are generally considered to be the first generation of American Yiddish poets—and his poetry became significant not only to what Wiener would soon call the history of Yiddish literature but also to the history of American literature more generally and of American immigrant, ethnic, proletarian literatures in particular. Like Wiener's translations of Peretz, *Songs from the Ghetto* included facing pages containing the Yiddish "originals" in transliterated and highly Germanized versions. It was an imprimatur by a respected Harvard scholar that brought attention not only to Rosenfeld's poetry but also to Yiddish. The realist novelist and critic William Dean Howells lauded the simplicity, the subtlety, and the realism of Rosenfeld's poetry (or, rather, of Wiener's translations).[9] Wiener's translation served Rosenfeld well and is properly credited with bringing the poet international fame.

To return to the century under consideration throughout this study, there is one final example to consider of the bolder, more sweeping claims that Yiddish authors tend to make and that English translators tend to mute. Glatshteyn's "A gute nakht, velt" was written before World War II began. At the end of the war, in 1945, Kadya Molodovsky (1894–1974) wrote a poem titled "El khanun," the Hebrew prayerful words for "God of Mercy."[10]

אל חנון

אל חנון,

קלײַב אויס אַן אנדער פֿאָלק,

דערווייל.

מיר זײַנען מיד פֿון שטאַרבן און געשטאַרבן,

מיר האָבן ניט קײן תפֿילות מער,

קלײַב אויס אַן אנדער פֿאָלק,

דערװײַל,

מיר האָבן ניט קײן בלוט מער

אױך צו זײַן אַ קרבן.

אַ מדבר איז געװאָרן אונדזער שטוב.

די ערד איז קאַרג פֿאַר אונדז אױף קבֿרים,

נישטאָ קײן קינות מער פֿאַר אונדז,

נישטאָ קײן קלאָג-ליד

אין די אַלטע ספֿרים.

אל חנון,

הײליק אַן אַנדער לאַנד,

אַן אַנדער באַרג.

מיר האָבן אַלע פֿעלדער שױן און יעדן שטײן

מיט אַש, מיט הײליקן באַשאָטן.

מיט זקנים,

און מיט יונגע,

און מיט עופֿהלער באַצאָלט

פֿאַר יעדן אות פֿון דײַנע צען געבאָטן.

אל חנון,

הײב אױף דײַן פֿײַערדיקע ברעם,

און זע די פֿעלקער פֿון דער װעלט —

גיב זיי די נבֿואות און די יום-נוראים.

אין יעדן לשון פּרעפֿלט מען דײַן װאָרט —

לערן די מעשׂים זיי,

די װעגן פֿון נסיון.

אל חנון,

גיב פּראָסטע בגדים אונדז,

פֿון פֿאַסטעכער פֿאַר שאָף,

פֿון שמידן בײַ די דעם האַמער,

פֿון װעש-װאַשער, פֿון פֿעל-שינדער,

און נאָך מער געמײנעס.

און נאָך אײן חסד טו צו אונדז:

אל חנון,

נעם צו פֿון אונדז די שכינה פֿון גאונות.

1945

As the full horrors of the times are being revealed, the poet asserts that it is time for the God of Mercy to give the Jews a rest. *"El khanun / klayb oys an ander folk,"* she writes: "God of mercy, choose another people."[11] The burdens of chosenness have become too much to bear, the poet asserts, and there are no more sacrifices that the Jews are capable of making.

Consider the two translations of the poem published by Irving Howe in 1969 and in 1987.[12] Like Marie Syrkin's translation of "A gute nakht, velt" ("Good Night, Wide World"), Howe's translation first appeared in *A Treasury of Yiddish Poetry.*

O God of Mercy	O God of Mercy
For the time being	Choose—
Choose another people.	Another people.
We are tired of death,	We are tired of death, tired of corpses.
tired of corpses,	We have no more prayers.
We have no more prayers.	Choose—
For the time being	Another people
Choose another people.	We have run out of blood
We have run out of blood	For victims,
For victims,	Our houses have been turned
Our houses have been turned into desert,	into desert.
The earth lacks space for tombstones,	The earth lacks space for tombstones,
There are no more lamentations	There are no more lamentations
Nor songs of woe	Nor songs of woe
In the ancient texts.	In the ancient texts.
God of Mercy	God of Mercy
Sanctify another land,	Sanctify another land
Another Sinai.	Another Sinai.
We have covered every field and stone	We have covered every field and stone
With ashes and holiness.	With ashes and holiness.
With our crones	With our crones
With our young	With our young
With our infants	With our infants
We have paid for each letter in your	We have paid for each letter in your
Commandments.	Commandments.

God of Mercy	God of Mercy
Lift up your fiery brow,	Lift up your fiery brow,
Look on the peoples of the world,	Look on the peoples of the world,
Let them have the prophecies and	Let them have the prophecies and
Holy Days	Holy Days
Who mumble your words in every	Who mumble your words in every
tongue.	tongue.
Teach them the Deeds	Teach them the Deeds
And the ways of temptation.	And the ways of temptation.
God of Mercy	God of Mercy
To us give rough clothing	To us give rough clothing
Of shepherds who tend sheep	Of shepherds who tend sheep
Of blacksmiths at the hammer	Of blacksmiths at the hammer
Of washerwomen, cattle slaughterers	Of washerwomen, cattle slaughterers
And lower still.	And lower still.
And O God of Mercy	And O God of Mercy
Grant us one more blessing—	Grant us one more blessing—
Take back the gift of our separateness.	*Take back the divine glory of our genius.*
—Translated by	—Translated by
Irving Howe (1969)	Irving Howe (1987)

In just these few highlighted differences (indicated in my emphasis above) between Howe's two versions we can trace the dramatic changes in translation theory, in American ethnic consciousness, and in American Jewish cultural security and assertiveness that have been the subject of this study.

In the nearly twenty years that separated Howe's translations, he made only two substantive changes. The first of these, the erasure of the line "For the time being," was simply a correction of an error made in the 1969 translation. Like the possible confusion that we have encountered before between Glatshteyn's *mayn* (mine) and *meyn* (meaning) or Margolin's *gayst* (spirit) and *geyst* (go, pass), Howe at first confuses the adverb *dervayl* (meanwhile, for the time being) with the imperative *derveyl* (elect, choose).[13] Meaning, as we have seen before, hangs on accent and orthography and a *pasekh*. As Molodovsky's reading of the poem makes unambiguously clear, she means *derveyl* and not *dervayl*. The speaker of this poem, in other words, is not equivocating about her desire to stop being one of the Chosen People. She is not anticipating a future return to chosenness after a time of mourning. She rejects chosenness entirely and for all time and, with it, the covenant between God and the Jewish people.

Howe's changes to the very last line of the poem are even more revealing. The last three lines of Molodovsky's poem are

Un nokh eyn khesed tu tsu undz:
El khanun,
nem tsu fun undz di shkineh fun gaonus.

Shkineh and *gaonus* pose problems. They are Hebrew, and again, as in Glatshteyn's poem, they have unmistakable religious resonance. A *gaon* is a genius—but particularly a brilliant student of Talmudic and religious teachings. *Shekhinah/shkineh* can be translated variously as "God's presence," "Divine Immanence," or "the glory (or radiance) of God"; in mystical thought, it is considered the feminine aspect of God that may be perceived by humans at particular times and places. A Yiddish audience would know that and would recognize the claims made by invoking God's presence and Israel's genius. These are proud words. They are defiant, and they make the rejection of chosenness all the more radical. Molodovsky rejects everything that sets the Jews apart, including the very God she addresses. When Howe first published the poem, he rendered this last line as "Take back the gift of our separateness." "Separateness" is much more tentative than "genius," a state of being (and not a particularly desirable one) rather than a claim to a certain kind of power and knowledge. And what we see is not God's radiance but the tamer "gift" he has bestowed. Addressing an American audience not yet claiming ethnic particularism or Jewish assertiveness, Howe offers a much more subdued view of the Jews, one that is considerably more modest than Molodovsky's own.

The changes made to this final line in 1987 are dramatic. "Take back the divine glory of our genius," Howe now writes, restoring the line to Molodovsky's Yiddish meaning.[14] By then, Howe seems more ready to assert Jewish genius and to claim it as divinely given. He may also have been more inclined to think that his readers would understand the Jewish resonance of "divine glory" or "genius" or that they should at least be compelled to think about them. In any case, readers are invited to pause over these lines, work at understanding them, perhaps even wonder what they meant in Yiddish and to Molodovsky.

What we have here—and, indeed, in all the considerations of multiple translations I have been tracing—are remarkable examples of historical and cultural processes at work. Different audiences certainly demand different understandings of the same text. But, more recently, we have also seen a surprising phenomenon: recent translations of Yiddish have been more faithful not only to the words of the Yiddish but to their boldness, their ambivalence about modernity and their embrace of it. As American Jews have gained in security and as American culture has become more ethnically diverse, there has been a clearer echo of the voice of defiance, of the tensions and the grappling with Jewish thought that we have seen in Yiddish texts. English translations were responding to and influenced by mass emigration, the loss of the Eastern European homeland, the creation of the State of Israel, and, most profoundly, the Holocaust. This certainly subdued the critique that had always been a hallmark of Yiddish literature.

It is worth acknowledging here that criticizing Yiddish translations has become something of a popular, if still minor, international sport. I have not wished simply to contribute to such attacks, satisfying though they may sometimes be. The aim has not been to offer "*fartaytsht un farbesert*" versions of any of these translations. Aesthetic sensibility, intimacy with at least two languages, cultural contexts, and even personal taste certainly demand our attention. We cannot, need not, resist reading translations through these lenses. But, like lenses, translations need to be adjusted every now and then to accommodate inevitable changes in how and what one sees. Taking into account developing theories about translation is one such adjustment. Considerations of intertextuality, multilingualism, and synergistic language contact are others. Still others include shifts in American ethnic consciousness, in Jewish histories, and in Yiddish as a spoken and written language. As we have considered shifting contexts, we have seen a renewed sense that translation should make the reader work for understanding, that there is no such thing as a seamless or "faithful" translation. We have also seen evidence of the growing assertiveness of Jewish identity in America, its return to the kinds of affirmations and denials that were possible in Yiddish when it was the spoken, common language of a large segment of the Jewish population in America. Writing for *eygene*—for one's own, one's people—made it possible to write unapologetically, asserting controversial ideas, experimenting with form, proclaiming one's presence. It took English translators some time to return to similar claims, now addressed not only to an intimate audience but to the wider world.

The questions posed by Sutzkever's poem at the beginning of this study—"*Ver vet blaybn, vos vet blaybn?*" (Who will last? And what? / Who will remain? What will remain?)—continue to haunt. Perhaps, after all, "last" connotes not finality, the last or end of something, but rather something that abides or continues, that lasts. The poet asks if God is the answer to these questions. He may be wondering if Yiddish can possibly be the answer. And we may continue to wonder if the answer lies not in any particular translation but in translation itself.

Appendix A

מאַריס תּפֿילה

גאָט, הכנעהדיק און שטום זיַינען די וועגן.
דורכן פֿיַיער פֿון זינד און פֿון טרערן
פֿירן צו דיר אַלע וועגן.

איך האָב פֿון ליבע געבויט דיר אַ נעסט
און פֿון שטילקייט אַ טעמפּל.

איך בין דיַין היטערין , דינסט און געליבטע,
און דיַין פּנים האָב איך קיין מאָל ניט געזען.

און איך ליג אויפֿן ראַנד פֿון דער וועלט,
און דו גייסט פֿינצטער דורך מיר ווי די שעה פֿון טויט,
גייסט ווי אַ ברייטע בליצנדיקע שווערד.[10]

109

"MARY'S PRAYER," TRANSLATED BY LAWRENCE ROSENWALD

God, these paths are poor and still.
Through fire of sin and fire of tears,
All paths lead to you.

Of love I have built you a nest,
Of silence, a temple.

I am your keeper, handmaid, and beloved,
And I have never seen your face.

And I lie at the edge of the world,
And you go darkly through me, like the hour of death,
Go like a broad and glittering sword.

"MARY'S PRAYER," TRANSLATED BY KATHRYN HELLERSTEIN

God, humble and mute are these ways.
Through the fire of sin and of tears
All ways lead to you.

I have built you a nest out of love
And out of silence, a temple.

I am your protector, servant, and beloved,
And I have never seen your face.

And I lie on the rim of the world,
And you pass through me, dark as the hour of death,
Pass like a broad, flashing sword.

God, meek and silent are the ways.
Through the flames of sin and tears
All roads lead to You.

I built You a nest of love
And from silence, a temple.

I am Your guardian, servant and lover,
Yet I have never seen your face.

I lie at the edge of the world,
While You pass through me darkly like the hour of death,
You pass like a broad, flashing sword.

Appendix B

JOSEPH LEFTWICH, *THE GOLDEN PEACOCK*, 1939

Good night, big world,
Great big stinking world.
Not you, but I bang the door and break off the latch.
With a long gabardine,
With a flaming yellow patch,
With proud step and mien,
At my own command I go
Back to the ghetto.
All apostate traces I stamp out, obliterate,
In your dust and mire I sprawl,
Praise, praise, praise,
Crippled Jewish life.
I bar your unclean cultures, world, I erect against them a wall.
Though you are waste and desolate,
I make myself dusty with your dust,
Miserable Jewish life.

Good night, world, you may keep for all it matters to me,
My liberators of humanity,
My Christs and Marxes and all they would do,
Keep the baptized blood they gave to you.
I have hope though he delay

113

Our redeemer will come one day,

And there will be

Fresh leaves upon our ancient tree.

I want no comforting, no pity,

I go back to my own city,

From Wagner's heathen music to my own Biblical chant.

Sad Jewish life, I kiss you,

I weep with the joy of coming back to you.

MOSHE SPIEGEL, *CHICAGO JEWISH FORUM*, 1967

Back to the crooked alleys and the flickering lamp wicks—

Good night, great world,

Huge, reeking world.

It is not you but I

Who slam the gate!

In pride and of my own free will,

In my long gabardine with its blazing yellow badge,

I go back to the ghetto.

I tread down all apostate traces.

I bathe in your dust,

O maimed Jewish life.

Back to my lighted kerosene and its shadows,

Back to the crooked alleys and the flickering lamp wicks,

Back to my Scriptures, my tractates of the Holy Law!

With my lantern I return once more

To the unending pilgrim search for truth and mercy.

I retreat with deep-felt joy

To the dim light of the ghetto.

Good night, world. I leave to you

Our mankind liberators;

Keep our Christs, and our Marxes,

And riot in the baptized blood of their aftermath.

Though God still tarries, still I cherish the hope

That one day He will show Himself once more;

One day, once more, green leaves will rustle

Upon the ancient tree.

I want no condolences;
Back to my house of refuge,
Back from the pagan Wagnerian thunder, to my single sacred chant
I will retrace my steps.
O bereaved Jewish life,
Bending crippled under your load of sorrow,
I weep for the joy of coming back to you . . .

RUTH WHITMAN, *DELOS*, 1968

Good night, wide world,
big stinking world.
Not you but I slam shut the gate.
With a long gabardine,
with a fiery yellow patch,
with a proud stride,
because I want to,
I'm going back to the ghetto.
Wipe away, stamp out every vestige of conversion.
I roll around in your refuse—
praise, praise, praise—
hunchbacked Jewish life.
Damn your soiled culture, world.
I wallow in your dust
even though it's forsaken,
sad Jewish life.

German pig, cut-throat Pole,
Rumania, thief, land of drunkards and gluttons.
Weak-kneed democracy, with your cold
sympathy compresses.
Good night, electrified arrogant world.
Back to your kerosene, candle shadows,
eternal October, minute stars,
to my crooked streets, humped lanterns,
my sacred pages, my Bible,
my Gemorra, to my backbreaking

studies, to the bright Yiddish prayerbook,
to law, profundity, duty, justice,—
world, I walk gladly towards quiet ghetto light.

Good night. I'll make you, world, a gift of
all my liberators.
Take back your Jesus-Marxists, choke on their courage.
Croak over a drop of our christianized blood.
For I have hope, even if He is delaying,
day by day my expectation rises.
Green leaves will yet rustle
on our sapless tree.
I don't need any consolation.
I'm going back to my very beginnings,
from Wagner's pagan music to melody, to humming.
I kiss you, disheveled Jewish life,
the joy of coming is weeping in me.

WHITMAN, *THE SELECTED POEMS OF JACOB GLATSTEIN,* 1972

Good night, wide world,
big stinking world.
Not you but I slam shut the gate.
With a long gabardine,
with a fiery yellow patch,
with a proud stride,
because I want to,
I'm going back to the ghetto.
Wipe away, stamp out every vestige of conversion.
I roll around in your garbage—
praise, praise, praise—
hunchbacked Jewish life.
Damn your dirty culture, world.
I wallow in your dust
even though it's forsaken,
sad Jewish life.

German pig, cutthroat Pole,
Rumania, thief, land of drunkards and gluttons.
Weak-kneed democracy, with your cold
sympathy-compresses.
Good night, electrified arrogant world.
Back to your kerosene, candle shadows,
eternal October, tiny stars,
to my crooked streets, humped lanterns,
my sacred pages, my Bible,
my Gemorra, to my backbreaking
studies, to the bright Yiddish prayerbook,
to law, profundity, duty, justice,—
world, I walk gladly towards quiet ghetto light.

Good night. I'll make you, world, a gift of
all my liberators.
Take back your Jesus-Marxes, choke on their courage.
Croak over a drop of our christianized blood.
For I have hope, even if He is delaying,
day by day my expectation rises.
Green leaves will yet rustle
on our sapless tree.
I don't need any consolation.
I'm going back to my very beginnings,
from Wagner's pagan music to melody, to humming.
I kiss you, disheveled Jewish life,
I cry with the joy of coming back.

MARIE SYRKIN, *A TREASURY OF YIDDISH POETRY*, 1969

Good night, wide world
Big stinking world!
Not you but I slam shut the door.
With my long gabardine,
My fiery, yellow patch,
With head erect,
And at my sole command,
I go back into the ghetto.

Wipe off all markings of apostasy!
I roll my body in your grime;
Glory, glory, glory to you,
Crippled Jewish life!
I cast out all your unclean cultures, world!
Though all has been laid waste,
I burrow in your dust,
Sorrowing Jewish life.

Swinish German, hostile Polack,
Thievish Amalekite—land of swill and guzzle,
Slobbering democracy,
With your cold compress of sympathy,
Good night, brash world with your electric glare.

Back to my kerosene, my shadowed tallow candles,
Endless October and faint stars,
To my twisting streets and crooked lantern,
To my sacred scrolls and holy books,
To tough Talmudic riddles and lucid Yiddish speech,
To law, to duty, and to justice,
To what is deeply mine.
World, joyously I stride
Toward the quiet ghetto lights.

Good night, I give you in good measure
All my redeemers;
Take your Jesus Marxes; choke on their daring,
Burst with each drop of our baptized blood.

And still I trust that though He tarry,
My waiting will spring newly day by day.
Green leaves again will rustle
On our withered tree.
I need no comforting.
I walk again my straight and narrow way:
From Wagner's heathen blare to Hebrew chant
And the hummed melody.

I kiss you, cankered Jewish life,
The joy of homecoming weeps in me.

SYRKIN, *THE LITERATURE OF DESTRUCTION*, 1988

Good night, wide world
Big stinking world!
Not you but I shut the gate.
With my long gabardine,
My fiery, yellow patch,
With head erect,
And at my sole command,
I go back into the ghetto.
Wipe off all markings of apostasy!
I roll my body in your grime;
Glory, glory, glory to you,
Crippled Jewish life!
I cast out all your unclean cultures, world!
Though all has been laid waste,
I burrow in your dust,
Sorrowing Jewish life.

Swinish German, hostile Polack,
Thievish Amalekite—land of swill and guzzle,
Slobbering democracy,
With your cold compress of sympathy,
Good night, brash world with your electric glare.

Back to my kerosene, my shadowed tallow candles,
Endless October and faint stars,
To my twisting streets and crooked lantern,
To my sacred scrolls and holy books,
To tough Talmudic riddles and lucid Yiddish speech,
To law, to profundity,
To duty and to justice.
World, joyously I stride
Toward the quiet ghetto lights.

Good night, I give you in good measure
All my redeemers;
Take your Jesus Marxes; choke on their daring,
Burst with each drop of our baptized blood.

And still I trust that though He tarry,
My waiting will spring newly day by day.
Green leaves again will rustle
On our withered tree.
I need no comforting.
I walk again my straight and narrow way:
From Wagner's heathen blare to Hebrew chant
And the hummed melody.
I kiss you, cankered Jewish life,
The joy of homecoming weeps in me.

ETTA BLUM, *JACOB GLATSTEIN POEMS*, 1970

Good night, vast world,
big stinking world!
It's not you, but I, who slam the door.
Stepping proudly in my long cloak
with its blazing yellow patch,
I return to the ghetto
of my own free will.
Erase,
stamp out all traces of apostasy!
Praise, praise, praise,
humpbacked Jewish existence!
I wallow in your filth.
Anathema, world, on your defiled civilization!
Wretched Jewish life,
laid waste as you are,
I immerse myself in your dust.

Swinish Teuton and vicious Pole,
Roumanian thief, land of gluttony and swill,
tottering democracy

with your cold sympathy compresses . . .
Good night, world, brazen electronic world!
I return to my kerosene and candle shadows,
to my perpetual autumn and minute stars,
to my crooked streets and humped lanterns.
I return to my tattered holy pages, the Bible,
to my Torah and the laborious learning,
to the glowing Sacred Language;
to the Law and the revealed exegesis,
to duty, to integrity . . .
With joy I pace to soft ghetto lights.

Good night, world.
To you I donate all of my liberators.
You may keep the Jesus-Marxes
and choke on their daring!
Croak on a drop of our apostate blood!
And, although He tarries,
day and night my waiting ascends.
Green leaves will yet stir
upon our barren tree.
I do not need your consolations,
I return to my rightful dwelling—
from Wagner's idolatrous music
to simple melody, to the Hebrew chant.
I embrace you, mangled Jewish life.
The joy of home-coming sobs in me.

> Written April 1938
> from *In Remembrance* 1943

BLUM, *WORLD JEWRY*, 1971

Good night, vast world,
big stinking world!
It's not you, but I, who slam the door.
Stopping proudly in my long cloak
with its blazing yellow patch,

I return to the ghetto
of my own free will.
Erase,
stamp out all traces of apostasy!
Praise, praise, praise,
humpbacked Jewish existence!
I wallow in your filth.
Anathema, world, on your defiled civilization!
Wretched Jewish life,
laid waste as you are,
I immerse myself in your dust.

Swinish Teuton and vicious Pole,
Amalek thief, land of gluttony and swill,
tottering democracy
with your cold sympathy compresses . . .
Good night, world, brazen electric world!
I return to my kerosene and candle shadows,
to my perpetual autumn and minute stars,
to my crooked streets and humped lanterns.
I return to my tattered holy pages, the Bible,
to my Torah and the laborious learning,
to the glowing Sacred Language;
to the Law and the revealed exegesis,
to duty, to integrity . . .
With joy I pace to soft ghetto lights.

Good night, world.
To you I donate all of my liberators.
You may keep the Jesus-Marxes
and choke on their daring!
Croak on a drop of our apostate blood!
And, although He tarries,
day and night my waiting ascends.
Green leaves will yet stir
upon our barren tree.
I do not need your consolations,
I return to my rightful dwelling—

from Wagner's idolatrous music
to simple melody, to the Hebrew chant.
I embrace you, mangled Jewish life.
The joy of home-coming sobs in me.

Written April 1938
from *In Remembrance* 1943

BENJAMIN AND BARBARA HARSHAV, *AMERICAN YIDDISH POETRY*, 1986; UNCHANGED IN *SING, STRANGER*, 2006.[*]

Good night, wide world.
Big, stinking world.
Not you, but I, slam the gate.
In my long robe,
With my flaming, yellow patch,
With my proud gait,
At my own command—
I return to the ghetto.
Wipe out, stamp out all the alien traces.
I grovel in your dirt,
Hail, hail, hail,
Humpbacked Jewish life.
A ban, world, on your unclean cultures.
Though all is desolate,
I roll in your dust,
Gloomy Jewish life.

Piggish German, hostile Polack,
Sly Amalek, land of guzzling and gorging.
Flabby democracy, with your cold
Compresses of sympathy.
Good night, world of electrical insolence.
Back to my kerosene, tallowy shadow,
Eternal October, wee little stars,

---

[*] In the later text, presumably due to a simple printer's error, two lines in the first stanza are run together: "Though all is desolate, I roll in your dust."

To my crooked alleys, hunchbacked street-lamp,
My stray pages, my Twenty-Four-Books,
My Talmud, to the puzzling
Questions, to the bright Hebrew-Yiddish,
To Law, to deep meaning, to duty, to right.
World, I stride with joy to the quiet ghetto-light.

Good night. I grant you, world,
All my liberators.
Take the Jesusmarxes, choke on their courage.
Drop dead on a drop of our baptized blood.
And I believe that even though he tarries,
Day after day rises my waiting.
Surely, green leaves will rustle
On our withered tree.
I do not need consolation.
I go back to my four walls,
From Wagner's pagan music—to tune, to humming.
I kiss you, tangled Jewish life.
It cries in me, the joy of coming.

    April 1938

RICHARD FEIN, *SELECTED POEMS OF YANKEV GLATSHTEYN*, 1987

Good night, wide world,
great, stinking world.
Not you, but I slam the gate.
With the long gabardine,
with the yellow patch—burning—
with proud stride
I decide -:
I am going back to the ghetto.
Wipe out, stamp out all traces of apostasy.
I wallow in your filth.
Blessed, blessed, blessed,
hunchbacked Jewish life.
Go to hell, with your polluted cultures, world.

Though all is ravaged,
I am dust of your dust,
sad Jewish life.

Prussian pig and hate-filled Pole;
Jew-killers, land of guzzle and gorge.
Flabby democracies, with your cold
sympathy compresses.
Good night, electro-impudent world.
Back to my kerosene, tallowed shadows,
eternal October, minute stars,
to my warped streets and hunchbacked lanterns,
my worn-out pages of the Prophets,
my Gemaras, to arduous
Talmudic debates, to lucent, exegetic Yiddish,
to Rabbinical Law, to deep-deep meaning, to duty, to what is right.
World, I walk with joy to the quiet ghetto light.

Good night. It's all yours, world. I disown
my liberation.
Take back your Jesusmarxists, choke on their arrogance.
Croak on a drop of our baptized blood.
And though He tarries, I have hope;
day in, day out, my expectation grows.
Leaves will yet green
on our withered tree.
I don't need any solace.
I return to our cramped space.
From Wagner's pagan-music to chants of sacred humming.
I kiss you, tangled strands of Jewish life.
Within me weeps the joy of coming home.

BARNETT ZUMOFF, *I KEEP RECALLING*, 1993

Good night, wide world,
Great stinking world;
Not you but I slam the gate.
With my long black coat

And my fiery yellow patch,
With a proud step
And at my own command,
I go back to the ghetto.
Erase and stamp out all traces of assimilation—
I am wallowing in your garbage.
Praise, praise, praise
O crippled Jewish life;
Anathema, world upon your unclean cultures.
Though everything is devastated,
I cover myself with your dust,
O sad Jewish life.

Pig of a German, hateful Polack,
Thieving Rumania, land of swilling and gorging;
Flabby Democracy, with your cold-compresses of sympathy.
Good-night, electricity-arrogant world-
Back to my kerosene, my tallow-candle shadows,
Eternal October, tiny stars;
To my crooked streets, humpbacked lanterns,
Torn old scrolls and Biblical studies,
Talmud and its difficult passages;
To glorious Yiddish,
To the sacred law, to deep meaning, to duty, to justice.
World, I stride with joy to the quiet ghetto lights.

Good night. I contribute to you, O world,
All my would-be saviors.
Take the Jesus-Marxes—choke on their courage;
Devil take you for a drop of our baptized blood.
And though the Messiah tarries,
My anticipation rises day by day.
Green leaves will yet rustle
On our withered tree.
I need no comforting—
I'm going back to my four walls,
Back from Wagner's pagan music to the humming of Hassidic
            melodies

I kiss you, O disheveled Jewish life—
The joy of coming back weeps within me.

ZACKARY SHOLEM BERGER, IN *LYRIC* AND ONLINE, 2004

Good night, world,
big stinking world.
Not you, but I slam the door.
With my long robe,
fiery yellow patch
and proud step,
at my own command
I'm going back into the ghetto.
Trampling baptismal traces.
I roll in your garbage.
Praise to you, praise, praise,
hunchbacked Jewish life.
To hell, world, with your polluted cultures.
Though everything is laid waste
I dust myself in your dust
sad Jewish life.

Swinish German, hateful Polack,
thieving Amalek, land of gorging and slobbing,
flabby democracy with your cold
compresses of sympathy.
Good night, electrified brazen world.
Back to my kerosene, candlestick shadows,
eternal October, minute stars,
to my crooked streets, hunched lanterns,
my stray pages, my twenty-four books
of Bible, my Talmud. Back to knotty
passages, to shining Yiddish glosses,
to judgment, deep intent, duty, justice:
world, I stride with joy to the quiet ghetto light.

Good night. To you, world, I donate
all my liberators.

Take the Jesusmarxes, choke on their bravery.
Die for a drop of our baptized blood.
I hope that though it tarries
my waiting will rise up daily.
Green leaves will still rustle
on our withered tree.
I need no comfort.
I'm going back to my four cubits,
from Wagner's idol-music to wordless tune and murmur.
I kiss you, shaggy Jewish life.
There weeps in me the joy of return.

Paris, 1938

Notes

1. TRANSLATION THEORY AND PRACTICE

Epigraph: Friedrich Schleiermacher, "On the Different Methods of Translating" (1813), trans. Susan Bernofsky, in *The Translation Studies Reader*, 2nd ed., ed. Lawrence Venuti (New York: Routledge, 2004), 59.

1   Avrom Sutzkever, Untitled, in *Lider fun togbukh: Poems 1974-1976* (Tel Aviv: Di Goldene Keyt, 1977), 16.

2   Avrom Sutzkever, Untitled (from *Poems from a Diary*), trans. Cynthia Ozick, in *The Penguin Book of Modern Yiddish Verse*, ed. Irving Howe, Ruth R. Wisse, and Chone Shmeruk (New York: Viking, 1987), 696.

3   Avrom Sutzkever, "Who will remain, what will remain? A wind will stay behind," in *A. Sutzkever: Selected Poetry and Prose*, trans. Barbara Harshav and Benjamin Harshav (Berkeley: University of California Press, 1991), 33. Reprinted by permission of the University of California Press.

4   Naomi Seidman, *Faithful Renderings: Jewish-Christian Difference and the Politics of Translation* (Chicago: University of Chicago Press, 2006), 14 and esp. 282n33. Seidman cites Michael Alpert's important work "Torah Translation," in *Routledge Encyclopedia of Translation Studies*, ed. Mona Baker (London: Routledge, 2001), 269–73.

5   Paul de Man reminds us that the German word *übersetzen* means "metaphor" (translating the Greek *metaphorein*, "to move over"), but "the translation is not the metaphor of the original" since that would imply a kind of resemblance or imitation of the original that is the mark of unsuccessful translations. De Man, *The Resistance to Theory*, Theory and History of Literature 33 (Minneapolis: University of Minnesota Press, 1986), 83.

6   The philosopher Friedrich Schleiermacher offered a similar distinction in German, using *Dolmetschen* to refer to speech, commerce, and diplomacy, where fidelity to the original can have serious consequences. Schleiermacher, "On the Different Methods of Translating," trans. André Lefevere, in *Translating Litera-*

ture: The German Tradition from Luther to Rosenzweig, by André Lefevere (Assen: Van Gorcum, 1977), 67–89. Most famously, Schleiermacher rejects this as a model for literary translation, repeatedly insisting that the reader and the reader's language must be made to grapple with the strange (source) language and remain estranged from it.

7   Jeffrey Shandler points to the amused interest generated "when New York City's Transit Authority programmed MetroCard vending machines in 2004 to offer Yiddish as one of the language options at selected subway stations in Brooklyn neighborhoods with large Jewish populations." Shandler, *Adventures in Yiddishland: Postvernacular Language and Culture* (Berkeley: University of California Press, 2006), 4.

8   Ibid., 4, 197. Shandler is neither celebrating this shift nor apologizing for it; he writes as a cultural historian and as an insider who has produced important scholarship and translations in, from, and about Yiddish.

9   Benjamin Harshav, *The Meaning of Yiddish* (Berkeley: University of California Press, 1990), 89–116.

10   See also Shandler, *Adventures in Yiddishland*, 116–25.

11   Peter Manseau, interview by Sarah Larson, The Book Bench, *New Yorker*, February 17, 2009, http://www.newyorker.com/online/blogs/books/2009/02/the-exchange-pe.html.

12   This expression, used in precisely the way I have used it here, is a colloquial way of saying that something is untrue or could not have happened. It invokes, not at all subtly or favorably, the Christian belief in Jesus's rising and ascension. As we will soon see in Isaac Bashevis Singer's *Gimpl tam,* such Yiddish dismissal of Christian beliefs is rarely translated.

13   Michael Stanislawski, e-mail communication, May 9, 2006.

14   De Man, *The Resistance to Theory,* 73. It is, by now, virtually impossible to discuss translation without considering Benjamin, but I proceed with the understanding that de Man's statement is a cautionary one.

15   Carol Jacobs, "The Monstrosity of Translation" *MLN* 90, no. 6 (December 1975): 758.

16   Walter Benjamin, "The Task of the Translator," trans. James Hynd and E. M. Valk, *Delos: A Journal on and of Translation* 2 (1968): 76. I use this less well-known translation because it is printed with facing German text, and I believe it is more readable than the more familiar translation by Harry Zohn found in Walter Benjamin, *Illuminations,* ed. Hannah Arendt (New York: Harcourt, Brace and World, Inc., 1968), 69–82. Zohn's first sentence is: "In the appreciation of a work of art or an art form, consideration of the receiver never proves fruitful" (69). Daniel Weissbort and Astradur Eysteinsson also chose to reprint the Hynd-Valk translation in their edited volume, *Translation—Theory and Practice: A Historical Reader* (Oxford: Oxford University Press, 2006), 297–309.

17   This is precisely what Schleiermacher urges translators to do: to subsume their own native fluency to preserve the foreignness of a text, to make readers feel that they are encountering something foreign. Schleiermacher, "On the Different Methods of Translating," trans. Lefevere.

18   First explored (in Hebrew) in his 1971 doctoral dissertation, Evan-Zohar's work appeared in English in his essay "The Position of Translated Literature within the Literary Polysystem," in *Literature and Translation: New Perspectives in Literary Studies*, ed. James S. Holmes, José Lambert, and Raymond van den Broeck (Leuven: Acco, 1978), 117–27; and, revised, in *Poetics Today* 11, no. 1 (1990): 45–51. The latter is widely reprinted.

19   See esp. Susan Bassnett, "The Translation Turn in Cultural Studies," in *Constructing Cultures: Essays on Literary Translation*, by Susan Bassnett and André Lefevere (Clevedon, U.K.: Multilingual Matters, 1998), 123–40; and Lawrence Venuti, introduction to *The Translation Studies Reader*, 2nd ed., ed. Lawrence Venuti (New York: Routledge, 2004), 43–63.

20   Benjamin, "The Task of the Translator," trans. Hynd and Valk, *Delos*, 76.

21   Ibid., 88. Zohn renders the same sentence as "The task of the translator consists in finding that intended effect [*Intention*] upon the language into which he is translating which produces in it the echo of the original." Benjamin, "The Task of the Translator," trans. Zohn, 76.

22   "Translation of an Epistle Addressed by R. Moses Maimonides to R. Samuel Ibn Tibbon," in *A Miscellany of Hebrew Literature*, ed. Albert Löwy (London: N. Trübner and Co., 1872), 1:219–28, quoted in Willis Barnstone, *The Poetics of Translation: History, Theory, Practice* (New Haven, Conn.: Yale University Press, 1993), 158. Barnstone attributes the quotation to Maimonides's *Guide for the Perplexed* rather than to the letter to his translator.

23   Barnstone, *The Poetics of Translation*, 21. Barnstone is here invoking Hans-Robert Jauss, the prominent reception theorist.

24   Renato Poggioli, "The Added Artificer," in *On Translation*, ed. Reuben A. Brower (Cambridge, Mass.: Harvard University Press, 1959), 147.

25   George Steiner, *After Babel: Aspects of Language and Translation* (New York: Oxford University Press, 1975), 396.

26   A fairly random, but quite representative sample, yields unsurprising affirmation of this critical claim. De Man in *The Resistance to Theory* (74), in comparing translations of Benjamin's German essay into English (Zohn's translation) and French, wrote that the essay was "impossible to translate." Emily Apter's twenty theses on translation begin and end with: "Nothing is translatable. . . . Everything is translatable." Apter, *The Translation Zone: A New Comparative Literature* (Princeton, N.J.: Princeton University Press, 2006), xi–xii. Derrida insists in *Monolingualism of the Other* (7) that every act is an act of translation and always from a foreign tongue: "We only ever speak one language. We never speak only one language."

27   *Letters of John Keats to his Family and Friends*, ed. Sidney Colvin (London: Macmillan and Co., 1891), 48; Harold Bloom, *The Anxiety of Influence: A Theory of Poetry* (New York: Oxford University Press, 1973).

28   Keats, in a letter to his brothers from December 22, 1817, defines negative capability as a state in which "a man is capable of being in uncertainties, mysteries, doubts, without any irritable reaching after fact and reason." *Letters of John Keats*, 48.

29   Frantz Fanon, "On National Culture," chap. 4 in *The Wretched of the Earth*, trans. Constance Farrington (New York: Grove Press, 1963), 231.

30   Max Weinreich, *The History of the Yiddish Language*, trans. Shlomo Noble (Chicago: University of Chicago Press, 1980), 164–67.

31   Cynthia Ozick, "Envy; or, Yiddish in America—a Novella," *Commentary* 48, no. 5 (November 1969): 33–53. Shandler writes in *Adventures in Yiddishland* (115n63) that, in a public presentation in 1999, Ozick offered a different explanation of the story's origins, claiming that she was describing not the plight of Yiddish writers who, by 1969, had found translators in America but, rather, that of Hebrew writers who had not and therefore had no readers outside of Israel.

32   Anna Margolin, "Maris tfile," in *Lider*, ed. and introduced by Avrom Nowerstern [Abraham Novershtern] (Jerusalem: Magnes Press, 1991), 96. Reprinted by permission of Magnes Press.

33   See the exchange about this poem among Kathryn Hellerstein, Lawrence Rosenwald, and Anita Norich in *Prooftexts: A Journal of Jewish Literary History* 20, nos. 1–2 (Winter/Spring 2000): 191–218. Hellerstein's and Rosenwald's translations are in these *Prooftexts* pages and are reprinted by permission of Indiana University Press. "Mary's Prayer," trans. Shirley Kumove, in *Drunk from the Bitter Truth: The Poems of Anna Margolin* (Albany: State University of New York Press, 2005), 189. Reprinted by permission.

2. HOW TEVYE LEARNED TO FIDDLE

1   The DVD "collector's edition" contains voice-over commentary by director Norman Jewison and actor Chaim Topol. In it Jewison reports that when the play was performed in Japan, Joseph Stein, who wrote the screenplay, was met with the following comment: "We know it's been successful here in Japan. But how is it they liked it in America?" "Audio Commentary by Director/Producer Norman Jewison and Actor Topol," *Fiddler on the Roof*, disc 1 of two-disc collector's edition (1971; Beverly Hills, Calif.: Twentieth Century Fox Home Entertainment, 2006). Seth Wolitz cites a slightly different version of this exchange in which the Japanese producer of *Fiddler* turned to Stein and said, "Tell me, do they understand this show in America?" When asked what he meant by that question, he replied: "It's so Japanese!" "The Americanization of Tevye or Boarding the Jewish *Mayflower*," *American Quarterly* 40, no. 4 (December 1988): 532. For several years after its initial appearance in 2006, an all-Japanese version made a much-discussed appearance on YouTube. See, e.g., "Japanese Fiddler on the Roof," 7:15, YouTube video, posted by Richie Sevrinsky, March 16, 2006, http://www.youtube.com/watch?v=eGoRo-nPLOM. For the Hindi version, see "Fiddler on the Roof (Hindi)," pt. 1, "Tradition—Parampara," 4:45, YouTube video, posted by Rakesh Kumar Gupta, March 25, 2008, http://www.youtube.com/watch?v=fcj86fzyoZE.

2   Michael André Bernstein, "Victims-in-Waiting: Backshadowing and the Representation of European Jewry," *New Literary History* 29, no. 4 (Autumn 1998): 625–51.

3   Ruth R. Wisse points out that "in contradistinction to most contemporary Euro-

pean literature, Sholem Aleichem wrote his masterwork about generational conflict from the *parent's* point of view" (emphasis Wisse's). Wisse, *The Modern Jewish Canon: A Journey through Language and Culture* (New York: Free Press, 2000), 47.

4   Literary analyses of *Tevye* are too numerous to name here. Among the most significant ones in Yiddish, see Nahum Oyslender (1893–1962), "Der yunger Sholem Aleykhem un zayn roman *Stempenyu*" [The young Sholem Aleichem and his novel *Stempenyu*], in *Shriftn fun der katedre far yidisher kultur bay der alukrainisher visnshaftlekher akademye* (Kiev) 1 (1928): 5–72; Meyer Weiner (1893–1941), *Tsu der geshikhte fun der yidisher literatur in 19tn yorhundert* [On the history of Yiddish literature in the nineteenth century] (New York: YKUF, 1946), 235–378; Baal Makhshoves (pen name of Yisroel Elyashev, 1873–1924), *Geklibene shriftn* [Selected Writings] (Warsaw: Kletskin, 1929), 1:91–109; and Y. Y. Trunk, *Tevye un Menakhem Mendl in yidishn veltgoyrl* [Tevye and Menakhem Mendl in Jewish world-destiny] (New York: CYCO, 1944). In English, see in particular Wisse, *The Modern Jewish Canon*; and Dan Miron, *From Continuity to Contiguity: Toward a New Jewish Literary Thinking* (Stanford, Calif.: Stanford University Press, 2010).

5   I am indebted to Seth Wolitz's essay "The Americanization of Tevye," which offers an authoritative comparison of *Tevye* and *Fiddler*. Ken Frieden examines the Yiddish, English, and Russian films in "A Century in the Life of Sholem Aleichem's Tevye," in *When Joseph Met Molly: A Reader on Yiddish Film*, ed. Sylvia Paskin (Nottingham, U.K.: Five Leaves Publications, 1999), 255–72; reprinted from *The B. G. Rudolph Lectures in Judaic Studies* (Syracuse, N.Y.: Syracuse University Press, 1997).

6   For a detailed view of the work's publication history, see Chone Shmeruk, " 'Tevye der milkhiker': Le toldoteha shel yetzira" ["Tevye the Dairyman": History of the work], *HaSifrut* 8, no. 26 (April 1978): 26–38. Although written as part of the Tevye cycle, the last two chapters were added to the collected tales in *The Complete Tevye the Dairyman* after Sholem Aleichem's death.

7   For an illuminating analysis of such quotations, see Michael Stern, "Tevye's Art of Quotation," *Prooftexts: A Journal of Jewish Literary History* 6, no. 1 (January 1986): 79–96. Stern argues that, far from being comical (though they can be quite funny), Tevye's quotations allow him to comment on and control the narrative. This volume of *Prooftexts* contains an excellent collection of critical essays about Sholem Aleichem, many of them translated from Yiddish.

8   In the Hebrew film, Chava's story follows that of Shprintse, as if to underscore its (greater?) significance.

9   Translations throughout are my own unless otherwise noted. Sholem Aleichem, *Tevye der milkhiker* [Tevye the Dairyman] (Warsaw: Kultur-Lige, 1921), 163. Subsequent citations refer to this edition and are indicated parenthetically in the text.

10 Yuri Slezkine suggests that each of Tevye's daughters represents a different destination: Russia (Hodl), Israel (Chava, presumably because she returns to her people), and America (Beylke). Slezkine, *The Jewish Century* (Princeton, N.J.: Princeton University Press, 2004), 203–6.

11 This chapter does not seek to compare the various translations of the text into English: *Tevye's Daughters*, trans. Frances Butwin (New York: Crown, 1949); *Tevye the Dairyman and the Railroad Stories*, trans. Hillel Halkin (New York: Schocken, 1987); *Tevye the Dairyman, and Other Stories*, trans. Miriam Katz (Malibu, Calif.: Joseph Simon / Pangloss Press, 1994), illustrated reissue of the work originally published in Moscow (Raduga Publishers, 1988); and *Tevye the Dairyman and Motl the Cantor's Son*, trans. Aliza Shevrin (New York: Penguin, 2009).

12 *Tevye*, directed by and starring Maurice Schwartz (1939; Waltham, Mass.: National Center for Jewish Films, 1989), DVD. Eric Goldman reports that, in 1936, Schwartz had hoped to film in Poland; three years later he chose a different site where he "felt that the topography of the region was almost identical to that of the countryside which Sholem Aleichem depicted." Goldman, *Visions, Images, and Dreams: Yiddish Film Past and Present* (Teaneck, N.J.: Ergo Media, 1988), 124.

13 In the voice-over that accompanies the DVD, both Topol and Jewison remind the viewer of the contrast between their experiences in Yugoslavia and the subsequent historical events that made that region infamous. They say that they would have been unable to predict or imagine the criminality and chaos of Bosnia or the Serbo-Croatian war. In Tito's Yugoslavia, they assert, they saw no sign of ethnic tension. The analogues to twentieth-century Jewish history are left unspoken.

Jewison had wanted to make the movie in Russia, but that proved impossible, presumably because the pogrom scene points too vividly to Russian anti-Semitism. Jewison and Topol, "Audio Commentary."

14 *Tuvya va-sheva' benotav* [Tevye and his seven daughters], directed by Menachem Golan (1968; [Neve Ilan, Israel]: Globus Group, n.d.), VHS.

15 The Internet Movie Database (IMDb) indicates that there was a German film titled *Tevya und seine Töchter* that appeared on German TV in 1962 (http://www.imdb .com/title/tt0352910). IMDb mistakenly translates this title as "Tevye and His Seven Daughters." (There is no "seven" in the film's title.) I have been unable to locate this version.

16 See Vincent Canby's review of the film, "A Village's Pogrom and Its Wider Resonances," *New York Times*, January 26, 1993.

Jewison, on the other hand, tells us at several points in his voice-over that, despite his name, he is not a Jew ("I'm a goy," he says), but he spent time in Israel in order to "get into orthodox family life." Jewison and Topol, "Audio Commentary."

17 When the film opened in New York, Canby's review ("A Village's Pogrom") pointed out that it "has a completely contemporary sensibility. . . . Mr. Astrakhan is less interested in Jewish culture than in the ways in which racism serves the purposes of nationalism."

18 Aleksandr Kuprin (1870–1938) is less well known to English readers than Babel is, but he was and remains one of Russia's most famous writers. He is often compared to Maxim Gorky (who appears in Sholem Aleichem's text and in several of the films but not this one) and Anton Chekhov, both of whom he knew. His fiction continues to be made into film.

19 On the collector's edition DVD, Jewison refers to Chagall's musicians as the source

of his fiddler. Jewison and Topol, "Audio Commentary." Isaac Stern played the music for the film.

20 Ibid.

21 Topol was only thirty-five years old when the film was made, but he plays (and is made up as) a very convincing older man. Sholem Aleichem was also thirty-five when he began writing the Tevye cycle. Jewison asked Topol to play the role of Tevye after he had seen the actor perform the role on the London stage (ibid.). (Topol was to play it again in London in 1995, this time with his daughter as Chava.)

22 Translations from the Hebrew are my own.

23 A more accurate number of Jews living in Russia at that time would be closer to five million: "The official (if still imprecise) figure in the 1897 census was 5,198,401 Jews living in the Russian Empire, including Congress Poland. . . . This number must be augmented by the nearly 3 million Jews who emigrated from the Russian Empire to the West from the 1870s to 1917." Michael Stanislawski, "Russia: Russian Empire," in *YIVO Encyclopedia of Jews in Eastern Europe*, ed. Gershon David Hundert (New Haven, Conn.: Yale University Press, 2008), http://www.yivoen cyclopedia.org/article.aspx/Russia/Russian_Empire.

24 Russkï portal [Russian portal], . (I am grateful to my colleague Mikhail Krutikov for this source.) According to the 2011 U.S. Consumer Price Index, this amount would now be the equivalent of a little over $500. "Seven Ways to Compute the Relative Value of a U.S. Dollar Amount—1774 to Present," MeasuringWorth.com, http://www.measuringworth.com/uscompare.

25 Dan Miron provocatively suggests that among the many other ways in which Sholem Aleichem resembles Tevye is that both are consummate, if wordy, storytellers; both are remarkably accepting of "Jewish passivity"; and, in that very acceptance, both embrace traditional Jewish tropes rather than those of modern secular culture. Miron, *From Continuity to Contiguity*, 362–402; Miron, introduction to *Tevye the Dairyman and Motl the Cantor's Son.*

26 It is also a striking instance of the changes in the Soviet Union between 1971, when Jewison went to Yugoslavia because he could not film a pogrom scene in Russia (see note 13 above), and 1991, when such scenes punctuate the Russian film. My thanks to Benjamin Pollak for drawing my attention to this shift.

27 Frieden points to these names in his analysis of the film in "Sholem Aleichem's Tevye," 265.

28 I am grateful to Mikhail Krutikov and Julia Bernstein for pointing out these details to me.

29 Ruth 1:16–17.

30 Jewison and Topol, "Audio Commentary."

31 Wolitz writes in "The Americanization of Tevye" (529), that "the *Fiddler* artists dared to defend the Diaspora and to legitimize the option for American Jews of accepting comfortably and consciously their 'Jewish-American' status. In short, Tevye upholds the authenticity of the Diaspora as a valid alternative to going to Israel. . . . It is the useless busybody, Yente, the matchmaker, who is sent off to

Israel in the play, for . . . she represents the 'dead traditions' which shackled Eastern European Jewish life."

32 Jewison and Topol, "Audio Commentary."

33 Frieden makes a similar observation about Pamyat in "Sholem Aleichem's Tevye," 265.

34 Meyer Weiner, "On Sholem Aleichem's Humor," trans. Ruth R. Wisse, *Prooftexts: A Journal of Jewish Literary History* 6, no. 1 (January 1986): 44.

3. REMEMBERING JEWS

Epigraph: Franz Rosenzweig, *The Star of Redemption*, trans. Barbara E. Galli (Madison: University of Wisconsin Press, 2005), 313.

1 Anita Norich, "The Family Singer and the Autobiographical Imagination," *Prooftexts: A Journal of Jewish Literary History* 10, no. 1 (January 1990): 91–107; Janet Hadda, *Isaac Bashevis Singer: A Life* (New York: Oxford University Press, 1997).

2 Yitzhok Bashevis, *Der sotn in goray: A mayse fun fartsaytns* [Satan in Goray: A tale of former days] (Warsaw: Bibliotek fun Yidishn P.E.N.-klub, 1935; repr., New York: Matones, 1943); trans. Jacob Sloan as *Satan in Goray: A Novel* (New York: Noonday Press, 1955).

3 Yitzhok Bashevis, *Di Familye Moskat* (New York: M. Sh. Sklarski, 1950); trans. A. H. Gross [with Maurice Samuel, Lyon Mearson, and Nancy Gross] as *The Family Moskat* (New York: Alfred A. Knopf, 1950).

4 "An Interview with Isaac Bashevis Singer," by Joel Blocker and Richard Elman, in *Critical Views of Isaac Bashevis Singer,* ed. Irving Malin (New York: New York University Press, 1969), 19. Singer worked with A. H. Gross on the translation until the latter's death; Maurice Samuel then assumed Gross's role.

5 Anita Susan Grossman puts the problem most succinctly when she reminds us that "it was not for his popularity among Yiddish readers that [Singer] won the Nobel Prize in 1978." Grossman, "The Hidden Isaac Bashevis Singer: *Lost in America* and the Problem of Veracity," *Twentieth Century Literature* 30, no. 1 (Spring 1984): 41.

6 Irving Saposnik, "Translating *The Family Moskat*: The Metamorphosis of a Novel," *Yiddish* 1, no. 2 (Fall 1973): 26–37.

7 Hadda, *Singer,* 129. Hadda's source is Isidore Haiblum, "The 'Hidden' Isaac Bashevis Singer," *Congress Bi-weekly* 37, nos. 13–14 (December 25, 1970): 33–34. Lamenting the abridgment of the novel in English, Haiblum writes: "If memory serves . . . I seem to recall his complaining that the publishers forced the change on him" (34).

8 Ruth R. Wisse reproduces this translation in her essay "Language as Fate: Reflections on Jewish Literature in America," *Studies in Contemporary Jewry* 12 (1996): 129. Wisse reports how she came by the twenty-two-line fragment of the poem: the sociologist Daniel Bell recited it from memory within the hearing of British writer Chaim Raphael, who then repeated it to the historian Lucy Dawidowicz, who in turn repeated it to Wisse. Wisse's essay also cites

Philip Roth's reinvention of the *pupik* image, which I go on to discuss in this chapter.

9   T. S. Eliot, "The Love Song of J. Alfred Prufrock," in *The Wasteland, and Other Poems* (London: Faber and Faber, 1941), 17–22.

10   "If asked at what point American Jewish letters gave notice of its independence from Anglo American modernism, I would cite the day Isaac Rosenfeld, with the help of Saul Bellow, composed a Yiddish parody of 'The Love Song of J. Alfred Prufrock.'" Wisse, *The Modern Jewish Canon*, 289. See also Steven J. Zipperstein, *Rosenfeld's Lives: Fame, Oblivion, and the Furies of Writing* (New Haven, Conn.: Yale University Press, 2009), 41–44.

11   Yitzhok Bashevis, "Gimpl tam," *Yidisher Kemfer* 593 (March 30, 1945): 17–20; Isaac Bashevis Singer, "Gimpel the Fool (A Story)," trans. Saul Bellow, *Partisan Review* 20, no. 3 (May/June 1953): 300–313.

12   Sidra DeKoven Ezrahi, *Booking Passage: Exile and Homecoming in the Modern Jewish Imagination* (Berkeley: University of California Press, 2000), 201.

13   Singer, "Gimpel the Fool," trans. Bellow, 313; Bashevis, "Gimpl tam," 20.

14   Chone Shmeruk, introduction to *Der shpigl un andere dertseylungen* [The mirror, and other stories], by Isaac Bashevis Singer (Jerusalem: Magnes Press, 1979), xxxv. Ruth R. Wisse, whose analyses of these texts have influenced my own, offers precisely this translation of *tam*. She writes: "'Gimpel Tam,' a rare example of the schlemiel figure in postwar Yiddish fiction, is more correctly if less adequately translated as simpleton." Wisse, *The Schlemiel as Modern Hero* (Chicago: University of Chicago Press, 1971), 60.

15   See also Wisse, *The Schlemiel as Modern Hero*, 16–24, 60–69. David Roskies also connects Gimpel to the *tam* in Nachman of Bratslav's tale: "Gimpel achieves goodness in his personal life by ignoring, then willfully rejecting, the evil and skepticism around him." Roskies, *A Bridge of Longing: The Lost Art of Yiddish Storytelling* (Cambridge, Mass.: Harvard University Press, 1995), 294.

16   Sally Ann Drucker calls "Gimpel the Simple" "a title perhaps too cutely alliterative." Drucker, "I. B. Singer's Two Holy Fools," *Yiddish* 8, no. 2 (1992): 35. Joseph C. Landis makes a similar point in "'Gimpl tam' and the Perils of Translation," *Yiddish/ Modern Jewish Studies* 14, nos. 2–3 (2006): 112.

17   Menachem Feuer and Andrew Schmitz go further, invoking the "poor Tom" of Shakespearean drama. In a creative leap from the Yiddish *tam* to the English *Tom*, they call Gimpel "as the original Yiddish has it, a Tom—simpleton." Feuer and Schmitz, "Hup! Hup! We Must Tumble: Toward an Ethical Reading of the Schlemiel," *Modern Fiction Studies* 54, no. 1 (Spring 2008): 105.

The King James Version translates Corinthians 3:18–19: "Let no man deceive himself. If any man among you seemeth to be wise in this world, let him become a fool, that he may be wise. For the wisdom of this world is foolishness with God." And Corinthians 4:10: "We are fools for Christ's sake, but ye are wise in Christ."

18   Wisse illuminates a different understanding of "fool" when she writes in *The Schlemiel as Modern Hero* (4) that "in an insane world, the fool may be the only

morally sane man." Bashevis distinguishes Gimpel from those other unlucky figures of Wisse's analysis (e.g., the heroes of the classical Yiddish writers S. Y. Abramovitsh and Sholem Aleichem) by giving him a different appellation. Janet Hadda goes further by offering an intriguing psychoanalytic analysis of Gimpel, pointing to his self-awareness, great capacity for love, and ability to live well in the world. She argues that "Gimpel is a successful man whose subjective reality is undaunted by circumstances that would overwhelm a less daring person." Hadda, "Gimpel the Full," *Prooftexts: A Journal of Jewish Literary History* 10, no. 2 (May 1990): 284.

19   Seidman, *Faithful Renderings*, 262. Hadda, in her "Gimpel the Full" (284), also argues against the reading of Gimpel as a "holy fool," as she writes that "in keeping with the *tam* instead of *nar* of the Yiddish title, Gimpel is not a suffering martyr [. . .] he is a true *tam,* a full and complete human being—if important criteria for wholeness include a large measure of love, respect, and financial comfort." Hadda also provides a bibliography of the "holy fool" readings (294n3).

Landis, in " 'Gimpl tam' and the Perils of Translation" (110), dismisses the holy fool connection, calling it "a highly dubious assertion, that seems to be borrowed by one critic from another, none of whom, one suspects, has a first-hand knowledge of Yiddish literature or of the Gimpel text in the original." He cites the critic Gershon Sapozhnikov, who had reminded his Yiddish readers that the biblical Job was described (in Hebrew) as "*ish tam vyasher*" (literally "a simple, upright man"; the King James Version translates this phrase as "a perfect and an upright man"; JPS renders it as "wholehearted and upright"). Sapozhnikov suggests that *tam* has a particularly Jewish nuance, a spiritual resonance that was difficult to translate into other languages. ("*Tam hot a spetsieln yidishn nyuans, s'iz a min gaystike kategorye, velkhe s'iz shver ibertsuzetsn in andere shprakn.*") Sapozhnikov, *Yitskhok bashevis-zinger: Der kintsler fun zind un tshuve* [Isaac Bashevis Singer: The artist of sin and atonement] (Buenos Aires: Alveltlekhn Yidish kultur-kongres, 1981): 71–72, quoted in Landis, " 'Gimpl tam' and the Perils of Translation," 111.

20   Hadda, *Singer,* 130. Also cited in Seidman, *Faithful Renderings*, 257.

21   Singer, "Gimpel the Fool," trans. Bellow, 304; Bashevis, "Gimpl tam," 18.

22   Seidman, *Faithful Renderings*, 258.

23   Although I read the line a bit differently than Seidman does, I am indebted to her analysis, which has informed my own. Seidman writes: "The insult to Christians (except perhaps in the 'affectionate' diminutive 'Yoyzl' or 'little Jesus') seems indirect at best. . . . [W]hen Gimpel seems to take at face value the proposition that Yoyzl had no father, the reader understands that Gimpel's naïveté extends beyond his wife's evasions to include even the 'absurdities' of Christianity. The reference is anti-Christian, then, because it assumes that the reader will see in it evidence of the extremity of Gimpel's foolishness: he is such a fool, the omitted line implies, that he believes the one thing that no other Jew has ever swallowed—that Jesus's mother Mary (like his wife, Elka) was a virgin!" Ibid., 258.

24   Hadda, *Singer,* 130, cited in Seidman, *Faithful Renderings*, 257. Seidman claims

that Greenberg omitted the line about Jesus in his dictation to Bellow, but she does not indicate a source for that claim.

25   Steiner, *After Babel*, 319–20.

26   Ibid., 298.

27   Soon after he was named a Nobel laureate, I interviewed the author. I asked him about other Yiddish writers (he dismissed all but his brother), about critics, literature, his life. As he was known to do, he interviewed me as well, asking why I was wasting my time getting a Ph.D. in order to teach literature. In a typical (and, I am now happy to say, unsuccessful) attempt to shock, he said, "Literature is like orgasm." When I resisted the impulse to ask the expected "why?" he provided the question himself and then explained, "Some things you just can't teach." Or analyze, he implied. It seemed quite beside the point to counter with current evidence—in both fields—to the contrary.

28   Much of the following discussion of this memoir is taken from Norich, "The Family Singer and the Autobiographical Imagination."

The text first appeared as "In mayn foters bezdn-shtub" in the *Forverts* (New York), February 19–September 30, 1955. It appeared in book form in 1956 as *Mayn tatns bezdn-shtub*, published by Der Kval (New York), and was reissued in 1979 by Farlag Peretz (Tel Aviv). Citations are taken from the latter edition and are indicated parenthetically in the text. An English version of the novel appeared in 1966 as *In My Father's Court*, translated by Channah Kleinerman-Goldstein, Elaine Gottlieb, and Joseph Singer, published by Fawcett (New York). Citations to the English are indicated parenthetically in the text. Four installments (dated August 13, September 23, September 24, and September 30, 1955) appear in the *Forverts* but not in the subsequent edition.

29   Singer later published four more of these chapters in *An Isaac Bashevis Singer Reader* (New York: Farrar, Straus and Giroux, 1971). He added a curious and rather mysterious explanation for the late appearance of these chapters, introducing them by indicating that they had been omitted from the translation of *In My Father's Court* "for technical reasons." Curt Leviant published a volume of stories culled from the pages of the *Forverts* titled *More Stories from My Father's Court* (New York: Farrar, Straus and Giroux, 2000).

30   Esther Singer Kreitman, *Deborah*, trans. Maurice Carr [Morris Kreitman] (New York: Feminist Press, 2004), 57.

31   Esther Singer Kreitman, *Der sheydim tants: Roman* [The dance of the demons: A novel] (Warsaw: Farlag Bzsoza, 1936), 68.

32   Anita Norich, afterword to *Deborah*, by Kreitman. The Feminist Press republished the Carr/Kreitman translation of *Der sheydim tants: Roman* as *The Dance of the Demons* (New York, 2009), which includes two biographical essays: "My Uncle Yitzhak" by Maurice Carr and "My Grandmother Esther" by Hazel Karr. Before the publication of her novel, Kreitman published Yiddish translations in Warsaw of Charles Dickens's *A Christmas Carol* (*Vaynakht* [Helios, 1929]) and Bernard Shaw's *The Intelligent Woman's Guide to Socialism and Capitalism* (*Di froy in sotsializm un kapitalizm* [S. Goldfarb, 1930]).

33 By 1936, Jews in traditional dress were forbidden to walk in Warsaw's Saxon Gardens, but the 1946 English text links that prohibition explicitly with the horror that has just ended. The Yiddish text has those dressed in modern garb strolling freely in the Gardens "as if they weren't even Jews" (*vi zey voltn gor keyn yidn nisht geven*). Kreitman, *Der sheydim tants*, 145. The English text has the unorthodox heading for the Gardens, "where a notice 'JEWS WEARING GABARDINES AND DOGS NOT ADMITTED' barred the way for others." Kreitman, *Deborah*, 137. More radically, the English text erases any sign of the German culture that had, by 1946, become synonymous with genocide. In English, Deborah takes great comfort in reading Russian and especially the verses of Pushkin (97), but in Yiddish (88) she is comforted and inspired by German's Gothic script and by Goethe's poetry. Norich, afterword to *Deborah*, 311. For other differences between the Yiddish and the English, see the afterword.

34 Kreitman, *Der sheydim tants*, 8.

35 Isaac Bashevis Singer, "Nobel Lecture, 8 December, 1978," in *Nobel Lectures: Literature, 1968–1980*, ed. Tore Frängsmyr and Sture Allen (Singapore: World Scientific Publishing Co., 1993), 163–65.

36 These sentences are missing from the printed version. The speech, in its entirety, can be heard online at Nobelprize.org, "The Nobel Prize in Literature 1978: Isaac Bashevis Singer; Nobel Lecture, 8 December, 1978," http://nobelprize.org/nobel _prizes/literature/laureates/1978/singer-lecture.html.

37 Isaac Bashevis Singer, *Nobel Lecture* (New York: Farrar, Straus and Giroux, 1979), 24–25. In this bilingual publication, this paragraph is indented.

38 Singer, "Nobel Lecture, 8 December, 1978," 164. The Yiddish text is not given.

39 "Interview with Isaac Bashevis Singer," 3–4, 6.

40 Irving Howe, *World of Our Fathers* (New York: Simon and Schuster, 1976), 457. The poet Yankev Glatshteyn wrote that it was "really puzzling that a writer so deeply rooted in the Yiddish language should find greater acceptance in the stranger's world than in his own. A story by Singer has a Jewish facade but, paradoxically, it reads better in English than in the original Yiddish." Glatshteyn, "Singer's Literary Reputation," in *Recovering the Canon: Essays on Isaac Bashevis Singer*, ed. David Neal Miller (Leiden: E. J. Brill, 1986), 145.

41 "Interview with Isaac Bashevis Singer," 19. See also Stephen H. Garrin, "Isaac Bashevis Singer as Translator: 'Apprenticing in the Kitchen of Literature,'" in Miller, *Recovering the Canon*, 50–57. Garrin agrees with the author's own critical assessment of his translation skills.

42 For a bibliography of these early translations (and other work), see David Neal Miller, *Bibliography of Isaac Bashevis Singer, 1924–1949* (New York: Peter Lang, 1983).

43 Isaac Bashevis Singer, "On Translating My Books," in *The World of Translation* (New York: PEN American Center, 1971), 110.

44 "Interview with Isaac Bashevis Singer," 19.

45 Ruth Whitman, "Translating with Isaac Bashevis Singer," in *Critical Views of*

Isaac Bashevis Singer, ed. Irving Malin (New York: New York University Press, 1969), 46.

46   Conversation with Irving Buchen cited in Buchen's *Isaac Bashevis Singer and the Eternal Past* (New York: New York University Press, 1968), xi. Seemingly in response to Singer's insistence on the importance of his English texts, Buchen began his study of the author with a provocative (and defensive) claim: "I decided to examine the works of Isaac Bashevis Singer in translation because Isaac Bashevis Singer decided to exist in translation" (ix).

47   Paul Kresh says that the story was written in Yiddish in the 1950s; Roberta Saltzman cites the 1963 Yiddish publication. Kresh, *Isaac Bashevis Singer: The Magician of West 86th Street* (New York: Dial Press, 1979), 10; Saltzman, *Isaac Bashevis Singer: A Bibliography of His Works in Yiddish and English, 1960–1991* (Lanham, Md.: Scarecrow Press, 2002), 47. Yiddish original: Yitzhok Bashevis, "Yentl der yeshive-bokher," *Goldene keyt* 46 (1963): 91–110; *Meyses fun hintern oyvn* [Stories from behind the oven] (Tel Aviv: Farlag Y. L. Perets, 1971). English translation: Isaac Bashevis Singer, "Yentl the Yeshiva Boy: A Story," trans. Marion Magid and Elizabeth Pollett, *Commentary* 34, no. 3 (September 1962): 213–24, and then widely anthologized; republished separately in 1983 as *Yentl the Yeshiva Boy,* trans. Marion Magid and Elizabeth Pollet, with woodcuts by Antonio Frasconi (New York: Farrar, Straus and Giroux, 1983); for the stage adaptation, see Leah Napolin and Isaac Bashevis Singer, *Yentl: A Play* (New York: S. French, 1977); and for the film, see Barbra Streisand, Jack Rosenthal, and Isaac Bashevis Singer, *Yentl: Screenplay* (n.p., 1981), and *Yentl: A Film with Music,* screenplay by Jack Rosenthal and Barbra Streisand (New York: Warner Home Video, 1983).

48   "I. B. Singer Talks to I. B. Singer about the Movie 'Yentl,'" *New York Times,* January 29, 1984. Singer writes: "I am sorry to say I did not [like it]. I did not find artistic merit neither in the adaptation, nor in the directing. I did not think that Miss Streisand was at her best in the part of Yentl. I must say that Miss Tovah Feldshuh, who played Yentl on Broadway, was much better. [. . .] Miss Streisand lacked guidance. She got much, perhaps too much advice and information from various rabbis, but rabbis cannot replace a director." And, further: "There is almost no singing in my works. One thing is sure: there was too much singing in this movie, much too much." He also responds to Streisand's rejection of his own script, stating that "I don't mean to say that my script was perfect, or even good. But at least I understood that in this case the leading actress cannot monopolize the stage. [. . .] The result is that Miss Streisand is always present, while poor Yentl is absent."

49   Ibid.

50   Naomi Seidman suggests that such cross-dressing not only provides a "spicy" sense of transgression but also highlights the positive side of sexual segregation: "a camaraderie, equality, and authenticity" imagined as part of the homosocial scene. "In cross-dressing fantasy," she argues, "if nowhere else in the architecture of modernity, the erotics of the heterosexual and the homosocial can meet and

marry." Seidman, "The Erotics of Sexual Segregation," in *The Passionate Torah: Sex and Judaism,* ed. Danya Ruttenberg (New York: New York University Press, 2009), 113.

51 Bashevis, "Yentl der yeshive-bokher," *Goldene keyt,* 99; Singer, "Yentl the Yeshiva Boy," *Commentary,* 217. I have underlined certain words and discuss them in the following paragraphs of my text.

52 Bashevis, Yentl der yeshive-bokher, *Goldene keyt,* 101; Singer, "Yentl the Yeshiva Boy," *Commentary,* 220.

53 Bruria, the female Talmudist always invoked in such discussions, is the prime example of such women; Bashevis refers to her in the story. Daniel Boyarin considers the relevant rabbinic texts and the figure of the female Talmudist Bruria, as well as the nineteenth-century "Maid of Ludmir," in his "Studying Women: Resistance from within the Male Discourse," in *Carnal Israel: Reading Sex in Talmudic Culture* (Berkeley: University of California Press, 1993), 167–96.

4. RETURNING TO AND FROM THE GHETTO

Epigraph: W. H. Auden, "The State of Translation," *Delos: A Journal on and of Translation* 2 (1968): 30.

1 Anita Norich, " 'Good Night, World': Yankev Glatshteyn's Ambivalent Farewell," chap. 2 in *Discovering Exile: Yiddish and Jewish American Culture during the Holocaust* (Stanford, Calif.: Stanford University Press, 2007). My understanding of the Yiddish poem is explored in that chapter, but the translations I consider here are not.

2 Yankev Glatshteyn, "A gute nakht, velt," *Inzikh* 8, no. 3 (April 1938): 66–67.

3 This reading can be found on the compact disc (CD) edited, produced, and distributed by Sheva Zucker, *The Golden Peacock: The Voice of the Yiddish Writer* (2001). Also to be found at "Yiddish Poem Read by Jacob Glatstein," YouTube video, 2:15, posted by "kalabusha," April 29, 2009, http://www.youtube.com/watch?v=MyxSmah3gZc.

4 Glatshteyn, "A gute nakht, velt," *Inzikh.*

5 Yankev Glatshteyn, "Good Night, World," in *American Yiddish Poetry: A Bilingual Anthology,* ed. Benjamin Harshav and Barbara Harshav, trans. Benjamin Harshav and Barbara Harshav, with the participation of Kathryn Hellerstein, Brian McHale, and Anita Norich (Berkeley: University of California Press, 1986), 305–7.

6 Yankev Glatshteyn, "Back to the Ghetto," trans. Joseph Leftwich, in *The Golden Peacock,* ed. Joseph Leftwich (London: Robert Anscombe and Co., 1939), 332–33; reissued in London (1944) and again in New York (Thomas Yoseloff, 1961); reprinted in Nathan Ausubel, ed., *A Treasury of Jewish Poetry* (New York: Crown, 1957). "Return to the Ghetto," trans. Moshe Spiegel, *Chicago Jewish Forum: A National Quarterly* 26, no. 1 (Fall 1967): 17; "Good Night, World," trans. Ruth Whitman, *Delos: A Journal on and of Translation* 2 (1968): 118–21; also in *The Selected Poems of Jacob Glatstein* (New York: October House, 1972), 59–60. "Good Night, Wide World," trans. Marie Syrkin, in *A Treasury of Yiddish Poetry,* ed.

Irving Howe and Eliezer Greenberg (New York: Holt, Rinehart and Winston, 1969; Schocken paperback edition, 1976), 333–35 (page numbers are to the 1969 edition); reprinted (with emendations discussed below) in David Roskies, ed., *The Literature of Destruction: Jewish Responses to Catastrophe* (Philadelphia: Jewish Publication Society, 1988), 374–75. "Good Night, World," trans. Etta Blum, in *Jacob Glatstein: Poems* (Tel Aviv: I. L. Peretz Publishing House, 1970), 48–49.

7 Yankev Glatshteyn, "Good Night, World," trans. Etta Blum, *World Jewry* 14 (1971): 18. The British publication has "stopping" instead of "stepping," and "electric" instead of "electronic." The more substantive difference is the restoration of "Amalek" in place of "Roumanian."

8 Yankev Glatshteyn, "Good Night, World," trans. Harshav and Harshav, *American Yiddish Poetry*, 305–7; also in Benjamin Harshav and Barbara Harshav, eds., *Sing, Stranger: A Century of American Yiddish Poetry; A Historical Anthology* (Stanford, Calif.: Stanford University Press, 2006), 453–54. "Good Night, World," trans. Richard Fein, in *Selected Poems of Yankev Glatshteyn* (Philadelphia: Jewish Publication Society, 1987), 100–103 (reprinted by permission of the University of Nebraska Press, the current copyright holder); "Good Night, World," trans. Barnett Zumoff, in *I Keep Recalling: The Holocaust Poems of Jacob Glatstein* (Hoboken, N.J.: KTAV, 1993), 2–5; "Good Night, World," trans. Zackary Sholem Berger, *Lyric: Poetry Review* 5 (Winter/Spring 2004); and on *Zackary Sholem Berger* (blog), February 18, 2004, http://zackarysholemberger.blogspot.com/search/label/Yankev%20Glatshteyn. (Berger's translation substitutes "Paris, 1938" for the correct "April 1938.") All the translations can be found in appendix B.

9 Alain Renoir succinctly states a perception encountered frequently in translation studies: "In most cases a translation will become obsolete within ten to twenty years, so that a new one will be needed periodically." Renoir, "The State of Translation," *Delos: A Journal on and of Translation* 2 (1968): 56.

10 Benjamin, "The Task of the Translator," trans. Hynd and Valk, *Delos*.

11 Benjamin's essay was first published in German in 1923 as a preface to his own translation of Baudelaire's "Tableaux Parisiens." The *Delos* essay indicates that "Illuminations by Walter Benjamin, edited and with an introduction by Hannah Arendt, is to be published by Harcourt, Brace and World, Inc. in 1968." (It actually appeared in January 1969.) Cited in Benjamin, "The Task of the Translator," trans. Hynd and Valk, *Delos*, 76. That translator, Harry Zohn, is not named in this announcement, but his translation, in the 1969 edition, is the one most commonly cited.

12 Joshua Fishman, "Mother Tongue Claiming in the United States since 1960," *International Journal of the Sociology of Language* 50 (1984): 21–99. See also, in an echo of the Sutzkever poem with which I began this study, Joshua Fishman, "Vos vet vayter zayn? Vos vet undz noch blaybn?" [What will be? What will remain for us?], *Afn shvel*, April–June 1983, 2–4.

13 Glatshteyn, "A gute nakht, velt," *Inzikh*; reprinted in *Gedenklider / In Remembrance (Poems)* (New York: Farlag Yidisher Kemfer, 1943), 41–42; also in *Kh'tu dermonen / I Shall Record* (New York–Tel Aviv: Bergen Belsen Memorial Press, 1967), 12–13.

14　From Isaiah 6:3: "Holy, holy, holy is the Lord of Hosts; the whole earth is full of his glory."

15　Glatshteyn, "A gute nakht, velt," trans. Harshav and Harshav, 305.

16　Harshav and Harshav, *American Yiddish Poetry*, 305. By 2006, that explanation is edited in Harshav and Harshav, *Sing, Stranger*. There the last phrase—"prefiguring the hope for their punishment" (453)—has been deleted.

17　Glatshteyn, "A gute nakht, velt," trans. Harshav and Harshav, 305.

18　The editor of *The Literature of Destruction*, David Roskies, adds an explanatory note indicating "line 28 corrected" (618n69). The correction affects two lines, erasing "mine" and substituting "profundity." "To law, to duty, and to justice, / To what is deeply mine" becomes "To law, to profundity, / To duty and to justice." The only other difference between the two versions is the substitution of "gate" for "door" in the poem's third line. Howe and Greenberg, *A Treasury of Yiddish Poetry*, 335; Roskies, *The Literature of Destruction*, 375.

19　The twelfth of Maimonides's thirteen Articles of Faith: "*Ani ma'amin be'emuna shlema / b'viat hamashiach. / V'af al pi sheyitmahemeiah, / im kol zeh ani ma'amin, / im kol zeh achakeh lo / bechol yom sheyavo*" (I believe with complete faith / In the coming of the Messiah. / And even if he tarries, I still believe, / I will still wait for him, / In every coming day). My translation.

5. CONCLUDING LINES AND CONCLUSIONS

1　In 1954, *The Field of Yiddish* listed fourteen translations of Peretz's story. Uriel Weinreich, ed., "Translations of 'Bontshe Shvayg' in English," in *The Field of Yiddish* (New York: Linguistic Circle of New York, 1954), 1:297. This list was updated half a century later by Leonard Prager. See Prager, "Perets' 'Bontshe Shvayg' Revisited (Part One)," *Mendele Review: Yiddish Literature and Language (A Companion to MENDELE)* 3, no. 13 (August 31, 1999), http://yiddish.haifa.ac.il/tmr/tmr03/tmr03013.txt. I consider only a representative sample of these translations here.

2　I. L. Peretz, "Bontsie Shvayg," in *Ale verk* [Complete works] (Vilna: Kletskin, n.d., ca. 1920s), 5:129.

3　I. L. Peretz, "Bontsie Silent," trans. Leo Wiener, in *The History of Yiddish Literature in the Nineteenth Century*, by Leo Wiener (New York: Charles Scriber's Sons, 1899), 332–53; "Bontzye Shweig," in *Stories and Pictures*, by I. L. Perez, trans. Helena Frank (Philadelphia: Jewish Publication Society, 1906), 171–81; "Bontche Shweig," in *Three Gifts, and Other Stories*, by I. L. Peretz, trans. Henry Goodman (New York: Book League, 1947), 23–30; "Silent Bontche," trans. Maurice Samuel, in *Prince of the Ghetto*, by Maurice Samuel (Philadelphia: Jewish Publication Society, 1948), 74–83; "Buntcheh the Silent," in *In This World and the Next: Selected Writings*, by I. L. Peretz, trans. Moshe Spiegel (New York: Thomas Yoseloff, 1958), 58–65; "Bontsha the Silent," trans. Hilde Abel, in *Selected Stories*, by I. L. Peretz, ed. Irving Howe and Eliezer Greenberg (New York: Schocken Books, 1974), 70–77; "Bontshe Shvayg," trans. Hillel Halkin, in *The I. L. Peretz Reader*, ed. Ruth R. Wisse (New York: Schocken Books, 1990), 146–52; "Bontshe Shvayg," trans. Eli Katz, in *The Three Great Classic Writers of Modern Yiddish Literature*, ed. Marvin

Zuckerman and Marion Herbst (Malibu, Calif.: Joseph Simon / Pangloss Press, 1996), 3:187–94.

4   For a fuller analysis of this story, especially within Yiddish culture, see Ruth R. Wisse, *I. L. Peretz and the Making of Modern Jewish Culture*, The Samuel and Althea Stroum Lectures in Jewish Studies (Seattle: University of Washington Press, 1991); Roskies, *A Bridge of Longing*; and Anita Norich, "From the Politics of Culture to the Culture of Mourning," chap. 4 in Norich, *Discovering Exile*.

5   Peretz, "Bontsie Shvayg," in *Ale verk*, 5:129.

6   See Susanne Klingenstein, *Jews in the American Academy, 1900–1940: The Dynamics of Intellectual Assimilation* (New Haven, Conn.: Yale University Press, 1991), chap. 2. (Although Klingenstein cites Wiener's *History of Yiddish Literature* as his first book, it followed the book of translations of Morris Rosenfeld's poetry by a year.)

7   He was also the father of Norbert Wiener, the brilliant mathematician who is credited with founding the science of cybernetics and who made enormous contributions to computer science and robotics. Like his father, Norbert Wiener was multilingual. His theoretical research may also be considered a kind of translation work, moving between biological systems and mechanical ones, natural phenomena and engineered devices. See the profile in the Notable Names Database (NNDB), http://www.nndb.com/people/229/000103917 (accessed June 7, 2009).

8   Wiener, *History of Yiddish Literature*, x.

9   See Marc Miller, *Representing the Immigrant Experience: Morris Rosenfeld and the Emergence of Yiddish Literature in America* (Syracuse, N.Y.: Syracuse University Press, 2007), chap. 1.

10   Kadya Molodovsky, "El khanun," in *Der meylekh dovid aleyn iz geblibn* [Only King David remained] (New York: Papirine brink, 1946), 3–4. (This volume of her poems begins with "El khanun.") Molodovsky can be heard reading her poem on the same CD that contains Glatshteyn's reading: Zucker, *The Golden Peacock*. Also to be found at "Yiddish Poem by Kadia Molodowsky," YouTube video, 2:16, posted by "kalabusha," July 31, 2009, http://www.youtube.com/watch?v=AiLn2EaoXGM.

11   Molodovsky, "El khanun."

12   Kadya Molodovsky, "God of Mercy," trans. Irving Howe, in Howe and Greenberg, *A Treasury of Yiddish Poetry*, 289–90; and also in Howe, Wisse, and Shmeruk, *Penguin Book of Modern Yiddish Verse*, 331–32.

13   Kathryn Hellerstein writes that "the Yiddish is ambiguous" and that the second meaning (*derveyl*/elect) was suggested to her by Avrom Sutzkever and the critic Avrom Nowerstern. Kathryn Hellerstein, ed. and trans., *Paper Bridges: Selected Poems of Kadya Molodowsky* (Detroit: Wayne State University Press, 1999), 532n144. Poem reprinted by permission of Wayne State University Press.

14   Hellerstein renders this line as "Deprive us of the Divine Presence of genius." She translates the poem's title as "Merciful God." Hellerstein, *Paper Bridges*, 353–55.

Bibliography

Alpert, Michael. "Torah Translation." In *Routledge Encyclopedia of Translation Studies*, edited by Mona Baker, 269–73. London: Routledge, 2001.

Apter, Emily. *The Translation Zone: A New Comparative Literature*. Princeton, N.J.: Princeton University Press, 2006.

Auden, W. H. "The State of Translation." *Delos: A Journal on and of Translation* 2 (1968): 30.

Baal Makhshoves. *Geklibene shriftn* [Selected writings]. Vol. 1. Warsaw: Kletskin, 1929.

Barnstone, Willis. *The Poetics of Translation: History, Theory, Practice*. New Haven, Conn.: Yale University Press, 1993.

Bashevis, Yitzhok (*see also* Singer, Isaac Bashevis). *Der sotn in goray: A mayse fun fartsaytns* [Satan in Goray: A tale of former days]. Warsaw: Bibliotek Fun Yidish P.E.N.-Klub, 1935. Reprint, New York: Matones, 1943.

———. *Di Familye Moskat*. New York: M. Sh. Sklarski, 1950.

———. *The Family Moskat*. Translated by A. H. Gross [with Maurice Samuel, Lyon Mearson, and Nancy Gross]. New York: Alfred A. Knopf, 1950.

———. "Gimpl tam." *Yidisher Kemfer* 593 (March 30, 1945): 17–20.

———. *Mayn tatns bezdn-shtub*. Tel Aviv: Farlag Peretz, 1979. Originally published serially as "In mayn tatns bezdn-shtub," in *Forverts* (New York), February 19–September 30, 1955. First published in book form as *Mayn tatns bezdn-shtub*. New York: Der Kval, 1956.

———. *Satan in Goray: A Novel*. Translated by Jacob Sloan. New York: Noonday Press, 1955.

———. "Yentl der yeshive-bokher." *Goldene keyt* 46 (1963): 91–110.

———. "Yentl the Yeshiva Boy: A Story." Translated by Marion Magid and Elizabeth Pollett. *Commentary* 34, no. 3 (September 1962): 213–24. Republished in book form as *Yentl the Yeshiva Boy*, with woodcuts by Antonio Frasconi. New York: Farrar, Straus and Giroux, 1983.

Bassnett, Susan. "The Translation Turn in Cultural Studies." In *Constructing Cultures: Essays on Literary Translation*, by Susan Bassnett and André Lefevere, 123–40. Clevedon, U.K.: Multilingual Matters, 1998.

Benjamin, Walter. "The Task of the Translator" (1923). Translated by James Hynd and

E. M. Valk. *Delos: A Journal on and of Translation* 2 (1968): 76–99. Reprinted in *Translation—Theory and Practice: A Historical Reader*, edited by Daniel Weissbort and Astradur Eysteinsson, 297–309. Oxford: Oxford University Press, 2006. Retranslated by Harry Zohn, in *Illuminations*, by Walter Benjamin, edited by Hannah Arendt, 69–82. New York: Harcourt, Brace and World, Inc., 1969.

Bernstein, Michael André. "Victims-in-Waiting: Backshadowing and the Representation of European Jewry." *New Literary History* 29, no. 4 (Autumn 1998): 625–51.

Bloom, Harold. *The Anxiety of Influence: A Theory of Poetry*. New York: Oxford University Press, 1973.

Boyarin, Daniel. "Studying Women: Resistance from within the Male Discourse." Chap. 6 in *Carnal Israel: Reading Sex in Talmudic Culture*. Berkeley: University of California Press, 1993.

Buchen, Irving. *Isaac Bashevis Singer and the Eternal Past*. New York: New York University Press, 1968.

Canby, Vincent. "A Village's Pogrom and Its Wider Resonances." *New York Times*, January 26, 1993.

De Man, Paul. *The Resistance to Theory*. Theory and History of Literature 33. Minneapolis: University of Minnesota Press, 1986.

Derrida, Jacques. *Monolingualism of the Other*. Translated by Patrick Mensah. Stanford, Calif.: Stanford University Press, 1998.

Drucker, Sally Ann. "I. B. Singer's Two Holy Fools." *Yiddish* 8, no. 2 (1992): 35–39.

Evan-Zohar, Itamar. "The Position of Translated Literature within the Literary Polysystem." In *Literature and Translation: New Perspectives in Literary Studies*, edited by James S. Holmes, José Lambert, and Raymond van den Broeck, 117–27. Leuven: Acco, 1978. Reprinted in revised form in *Poetics Today* 11, no. 1 (1990): 45–51.

Ezrahi, Sidra DeKoven. *Booking Passage: Exile and Homecoming in the Modern Jewish Imagination*. Berkeley: University of California Press, 2000.

Fanon, Frantz. "On National Culture." Chap. 4 in *The Wretched of the Earth*. Translated by Constance Farrington. New York: Grove Press, 1963.

Feuer, Menachem, and Andrew Schmitz. "Hup! Hup! We Must Tumble: Toward an Ethical Reading of the Schlemiel." *Modern Fiction Studies* 54, no. 1 (Spring 2008): 91–114.

Fishman, Joshua. "Mother Tongue Claiming in the United States since 1960." *International Journal of the Sociology of Language* 50 (1984): 21–99.

———. "Vos vet vayter zayn? Vos vet undz nokh blaybn?" [What will be? What will remain of us?]. *Afn shvel*, April–June 1983, 2–4.

Frieden, Ken. "A Century in the Life of Sholem Aleichem's *Tevye*." In *When Joseph Met Molly: A Reader on Yiddish Film*, edited by Sylvia Paskin, 255–72. Nottingham, U.K.: Five Leaves Publications, 1999. Reprinted from *The B. G. Rudolph Lectures in Judaic Studies*. Syracuse, N.Y.: Syracuse University Press, 1997.

Garrin, Stephen H. "Isaac Bashevis Singer as Translator: 'Apprenticing in the Kitchen of Literature.'" In *Recovering the Canon: Essays on Isaac Bashevis Singer*, edited by David Neal Miller, 50–57. Leiden: E. J. Brill, 1986.

Glatshteyn, Yankev. "A gute nakht, velt." *Inzikh* 8, no. 3 (April 1938): 66–67. Reprinted in *Gedenklider / In Remembrance (Poems)*. New York: Farlag Yidisher Kemfer, 1943.

Also reprinted in *Kh'tu dermonen / I Shall Record*. New York–Tel Aviv: Bergen Belsen Memorial Press, 1967.

TRANSLATIONS

Berger, Zackary Sholem. "Good Night, World." *Lyric: Poetry Review* 5 (Winter/ Spring 2004). Also available at *Zackary Sholem Berger* (blog). February 18, 2004. http://zackarysholemberger.blogspot.com/search/label/Yankev%20Glatshteyn.

Blum, Etta. "Good Night, World." In *Jacob Glatstein: Poems*, 48–49. Tel Aviv: I. L. Peretz Publishing House, 1970. Reprinted with emendations in *World Jewry* 14 (1971): 18.

Fein, Richard. "Good Night, World." In *Selected Poems of Yankev Glatshteyn*, 100–103. Philadelphia: Jewish Publication Society, 1987.

Harshav, Benjamin, and Barbara Harshav. With the participation of Kathryn Hellerstein, Brian McHale, and Anita Norich. "Good Night, World." In *American Yiddish Poetry: A Bilingual Anthology*, edited by Benjamin Harshav and Barbara Harshav, 305–7. Berkeley: University of California Press, 1986. Reprinted in *Sing, Stranger: A Century of American Yiddish Poetry: A Historical Anthology*, edited by Benjamin Harshav and Barbara Harshav, 453–54. Stanford, Calif.: Stanford University Press, 2006.

Leftwich, Joseph. "Back to the Ghetto." In *The Golden Peacock*, edited by Joseph Leftwich, 332–33. London: Robert Anscombe and Co., 1939. Reissued in London in 1944 and again in New York by Thomas Yoseloff, 1961. Reprinted in *A Treasury of Jewish Poetry*, edited by Nathan Ausubel. New York: Crown, 1957.

Spiegel, Moshe. "Return to the Ghetto." *Chicago Jewish Forum: A National Quarterly* 26, no. 1 (Fall 1967): 17.

Syrkin, Marie. "Good Night, Wide World." In *A Treasury of Yiddish Poetry*, edited by Irving Howe and Eliezer Greenberg, 333–35. New York: Holt, Rinehart and Winston, 1969. (Schocken paperback edition, 1976.) Reprinted with emendations in *The Literature of Destruction: Jewish Responses to Catastrophe*, edited by David Roskies, 374–75. Philadelphia: Jewish Publication Society, 1988.

Whitman, Ruth. "Good Night, World." *Delos: A Journal on and of Translation* 2 (1968): 118–21. Also published, in a slightly revised version, in *The Selected Poems of Jacob Glatstein*, translated by Ruth Whitman, 59–60. New York: October House, 1972.

Zumoff, Barnett. "Good Night, World." In *I Keep Recalling: The Holocaust Poems of Jacob Glatstein*, 2–5. Hoboken, N.J.: KTAV, 1993.

———. "Di freyd fun yidishn vort." In *Di freyd fun yidishn vort* [The joy of the Yiddish word]. New York: Der Kval, 1961.

———. "Singer's Literary Reputation." In *Recovering the Canon: Essays on Isaac Bashevis Singer*, edited by David Neal Miller, 145–48. Leiden: E. J. Brill, 1986.

Goldman, Eric. *Visions, Images, and Dreams: Yiddish Film Past and Present*. Teaneck, N.J.: Ergo Media, 1988.

Grossman, Anita Susan. "The Hidden Isaac Bashevis Singer: *Lost in America* and the Problem of Veracity." *Twentieth Century Literature* 30, no. 1 (Spring 1984): 30–45.

Hadda, Janet. "Gimpel the Full." *Prooftexts: A Journal of Jewish Literary History* 10, no. 2 (May 1990): 283–95.

———. *Isaac Bashevis Singer: A Life*. New York: Oxford University Press, 1997.

Haiblum, Isidore. "The 'Hidden' Isaac Bashevis Singer." *Congress Bi-weekly* 37, nos. 13–14 (December 25, 1970): 33–34.

Harshav, Benjamin. *The Meaning of Yiddish*. Berkeley: University of California Press, 1990.

Hellerstein, Kathryn. "Translating as a Feminist: Reconceiving Anna Margolin." *Prooftexts: A Journal of Jewish Literary History* 20, nos. 1–2 (Winter/Spring 2000): 191–218.

Howe, Irving. *World of Our Fathers*. New York: Simon and Schuster, 1976.

Jacobs, Carol. "The Monstrosity of Translation." *MLN* 90, no. 6 (December 1975): 755–66.

Jewison, Norman, and Chaim Topol. "Audio Commentary by Director/Producer Norman Jewison and Actor Topol." Disc 1, *Fiddler on the Roof*. Two-disc collector's edition. DVD. Beverly Hills, Calif.: Twentieth Century Fox Home Entertainment, 2006.

Keats, John. John Keats to George and Thomas Keats, December 22, 1817. In *Letters of John Keats to his Family and Friends*. Edited by Sidney Colvin. London: Macmillan and Co., 1891.

Klingenstein, Susanne. *Jews in the American Academy, 1900–1940: The Dynamics of Intellectual Assimilation*. New Haven, Conn.: Yale University Press, 1991.

Kreitman, Esther Singer. *Der sheydim tants: Roman*. Warsaw: Farlag Bzsoza, 1936. Translated by Maurice Carr as *Deborah: A Novel*. London: Foyle, 1946. Republished as *The Dance of the Demons*. New York: Feminist Press, 2009.

———, trans. *Di froy in sotsializm un kapitalizm*. Warsaw: S. Goldfarb, 1930. Original: *The Intelligent Woman's Guide to Socialism and Capitalism*, by Bernard Shaw (1928).

———, trans. *Vaynakht*. Warsaw: Helios, 1929. Original: *A Christmas Carol*, by Charles Dickens (1843).

Kresh, Paul. *Isaac Bashevis Singer: The Magician of West 86th Street*. New York: Dial Press, 1979.

Landis, Joseph C. " 'Gimpl tam' and the Perils of Translation." *Yiddish/Modern Jewish Studies* 14, nos. 2–3 (2006): 110–15.

Maimonides, Moses. "Translation of an Epistle Addressed by R. Moses Maimonides to R. Samuel Ibn Tibbon." In *A Miscellany of Hebrew Literature*. Edited by Albert Löwy, 1:219–28. London: N. Trübner and Co., 1872.

Manseau, Peter. Interview by Sarah Larson. The Book Bench. *New Yorker*, February 17, 2009. http://www.newyorker.com/online/blogs/books/2009/02/the-exchange-pe .html.

Margolin, Anna. "Maris tfile." In *Lider*, edited and introduced by Avrom Nowerstern [Abraham Novershtern], 96. Jerusalem: Magnes Press, 1991.

TRANSLATIONS

Hellerstein, Kathryn. "Mary's Prayer." In "Translating as a Feminist: Response." *Prooftexts: A Journal of Jewish Literary History* 20, nos. 1–2 (Winter/Spring 2000): 199.

Kumove, Shirley. "Mary's Prayer." In *Drunk from the Bitter Truth: The Poems of Anna Margolin*, 189. Albany: State University of New York Press, 2005.

Rosenwald, Lawrence. "Mary's Prayer." In "Translating as a Feminist: Response." *Prooftexts: A Journal of Jewish Literary History* 20, nos. 1–2 (Winter/Spring 2000): 198.

Miller, David Neal. *Bibliography of Isaac Bashevis Singer, 1924–1949*. New York: Peter Lang, 1983.

Miller, Marc. *Representing the Immigrant Experience: Morris Rosenfeld and the Emergence of Yiddish Literature in America*. Syracuse, N.Y.: Syracuse University Press, 2007.

Miron, Dan. *From Continuity to Contiguity: Toward a New Jewish Literary Thinking*. Stanford, Calif.: Stanford University Press, 2010.

———. Introduction to *Tevye the Dairyman and Motl the Cantor's Son*, by Sholem Aleichem, ix–xxxvi. Translated by Aliza Shevrin. New York: Penguin, 2009.

Molodovsky, Kadya. "El khanun." In *Der meylekh dovid aleyn iz geblibn* [Only King David remained], 3–4. New York: Papirine brink, 1946.

TRANSLATIONS

Hellerstein, Kathryn. "Merciful God." In *Paper Bridges: Selected Poems of Kadya Molodowsky*, edited by Kathryn Hellerstein, 353–55. Detroit: Wayne State University Press, 1999.

Howe, Irving Howe. "God of Mercy." In *A Treasury of Yiddish Poetry*, edited by Irving Howe and Eliezer Greenberg, 289–90. New York: Holt, Rinehart and Winston, 1969. Revised version in *The Penguin Book of Modern Yiddish Verse*, edited by Irving Howe, Ruth R. Wisse, and Chone Shmeruk, 331–32. New York: Viking, 1987.

Nabokov, Vladimir. "On Translating 'Eugene Onegin.'" *New Yorker*, January 8, 1955.

Napolin, Leah, and Isaac Bashevis Singer. *Yentl: A Play*. New York: S. French, 1977.

Norich, Anita. Afterword to *Deborah*, by Esther Singer Kreitman, 299–315. Translated by Maurice Carr [Morris Kreitman]. New York: Feminist Press, 2004.

———. *Discovering Exile: Yiddish and Jewish American Culture during the Holocaust*. Stanford, Calif.: Stanford University Press, 2007.

———. "The Family Singer and the Autobiographical Imagination." *Prooftexts: A Journal of Jewish Literary History* 10, no. 1 (January 1990): 91–107.

———. "Translating as a Feminist: Response." *Prooftexts: A Journal of Jewish Literary History* 20, nos. 1–2 (Winter/Spring 2000): 191–218.

Oyslender, Nahum. "Der yunger Sholem Aleykhem un zayn roman *Stempenyu*" [The young Sholem Aleichem and his novel *Stempenyu*]. In *Shriftn fun der katedre far yidisher kultur bay der alukrainisher visnshaftlekher akademye* (Kiev) 1 (1928): 5–72.

Ozick, Cynthia. "Envy; or, Yiddish in America—a Novella." *Commentary* 48, no. 5 (November 1969): 33–53.

Peretz, I. L. [Y. L. Peretz]. "Bontsie Shvayg." In *Ale verk* [Collected works], 5:118–29. Vilna: Kletskin, n.d., ca. 1920s.

TRANSLATIONS

Abel, Hilde. "Bontsha the Silent." In *Selected Stories*, by I. L. Peretz, edited by Irving Howe and Eliezer Greenberg, 70–77. New York: Schocken Books, 1974.

Frank, Helena. "Bontzye Shweig." In *Stories and Pictures*, by I. L. Peretz, 171–81. Philadelphia: Jewish Publication Society, 1906.

Goodman, Henry. "Bontche Shweig." In *Three Gifts, and Other Stories*, by I. L. Peretz, 23–30. New York: Book League, 1947.

Halkin, Hillel. "Bontshe Shvayg." In *The I. L. Peretz Reader*, edited by Ruth R. Wisse, 146–52. New York: Schocken Books, 1990.

Katz, Eli. "Bontshe Shvayg." In *The Three Great Classic Writers of Modern Yiddish Literature*, edited by Marvin Zuckerman and Marion Herbst, 3:187–94. Malibu, Calif.: Joseph Simon / Pangloss Press, 1996.

Samuel, Maurice. "Silent Bontche." In *Prince of the Ghetto*, by Maurice Samuel, 74–83. Philadelphia: Jewish Publication Society, 1948.

Spiegel. Moshe. "Buntcheh the Silent." In *In This World and the Next: Selected Writings*, by I. L. Peretz, 58–65. New York: Thomas Yoseloff, 1958.

Wiener, Leo. "Bontsie Silent." In *The History of Yiddish Literature in the Nineteenth Century*, by Leo Wiener, 332–53. New York: Charles Scriber's Sons, 1899.

Poggioli, Renato. "The Added Artificer." In *On Translation*, edited by Reuben A. Brower, 137–47. Cambridge, Mass.: Harvard University Press, 1959.

Prager, Leonard. "Perets' 'Bontshe Shvayg' Revisited (Part One)." *Mendele Review: Yiddish Literature and Language (A Companion to MENDELE)* 3, no. 13 (August 31, 1999). http://yiddish.haifa.ac.il/tmr/tmr03/tmr03013.txt.

Renoir, Alain. "The State of Translation." *Delos: A Journal on and of Translation* 2 (1968): 55–57.

Rosenwald, Lawrence. "Translating as a Feminist: Response." *Prooftexts: A Journal of Jewish Literary History* 20, nos. 1–2 (Winter/Spring 2000): 191–218.

Rosenzweig, Franz. *The Star of Redemption*. Translated by Barbara E. Galli. Madison: University of Wisconsin Press, 2005.

Roskies, David. *A Bridge of Longing: The Lost Art of Yiddish Storytelling*. Cambridge, Mass.: Harvard University Press, 1995.

Saltzman, Roberta. *Isaac Bashevis Singer: A Bibliography of His Works in Yiddish and English, 1960–1991*. Lanham, Md.: Scarecrow Press, 2002.

Saposnik, Irving. "Translating *The Family Moskat*: The Metamorphosis of a Novel." *Yiddish* 1, no. 2 (Fall 1973): 26–37.

Sapozhnikov, Gershon. *Yitskhok Bashevis-Zinger: Der kintsler fun zind un tshuve* [Isaac Bashevis Singer: The artist of sin and atonement]. Buenos Aires: Alveltlekhn Yidish kultur-kongres, 1981.

Schleiermacher, Friedrich. "On the Different Methods of Translating." 1813. In *Translating Literature: The German Tradition from Luther to Rosenzweig*, translated and edited by André Lefevere, 67–89. Assen: Van Gorcum, 1977. Retranslated by Susan Bernofsky. In *The Translation Studies Reader*. 2nd ed. Edited by Lawrence Venuti, 43–63. New York: Routledge, 2004.

Seidman, Naomi. "The Erotics of Sexual Segregation." In *The Passionate Torah: Sex and Judaism*, edited by Danya Ruttenberg, 107–15. New York: New York University Press, 2009.

———. *Faithful Renderings: Jewish-Christian Difference and the Politics of Translation.* Chicago: University of Chicago Press, 2006.

Shandler, Jeffrey. *Adventures in Yiddishland: Postvernacular Language and Culture.* Berkeley: University of California Press, 2006.

Shmeruk, Chone. Introduction to *Der shpigl un andere dertseylungen* [The mirror, and other stories], by Isaac Bashevis Singer, v–xxxv. Jerusalem: Magnes Press, 1979.

———. " 'Tevye der milkhiker': Le toldoteha shel yetsira" ["Tevye the Dairyman": History of the work]. *HaSifrut* 8, no. 26 (April 1978): 26–38.

Sholem Aleichem. *Tevye der milkhiker* [Tevye the Dairyman]. Warsaw: Kultur-Lige, 1921.

TRANSLATIONS

———. *Tevye the Dairyman and Motl the Cantor's Son.* Translated by Aliza Shevrin. New York: Penguin, 2009.

———. *Tevye the Dairyman, and Other Stories.* Translated by Miriam Katz. Illustrated by Manuel Bennett. Malibu, Calif.: Joseph Simon / Pangloss Press, 1994. Originally published without illustrations in Moscow, by Raduga Publishers, 1988.

———. *Tevye's Daughters.* Translated by Frances Butwin. New York: Crown, 1949.

Singer, Isaac Bashevis (*see also* Bashevis, Yitzhok). "Gimpel the Fool (A Story)." Translated by Saul Bellow. *Partisan Review* 20, no. 3 (May/June 1953): 300–313.

———. "I. B. Singer Talks to I. B. Singer about the Movie 'Yentl.' " *New York Times,* January 29, 1984.

———. *In My Father's Court.* Translated by Channah Kleinerman-Goldstein, Elaine Gottlieb, and Joseph Singer. New York: Fawcett, 1966.

———. "An Interview with Isaac Bashevis Singer." By Joel Blocker and Richard Elman. In *Critical Views of Isaac Bashevis Singer*, edited by Irving Malin, 3–26. New York: New York University Press, 1969. First published in *Commentary* 36, no. 5 (November 1963): 364–72.

———. *An Isaac Bashevis Singer Reader.* New York: Farrar, Straus and Giroux, 1971.

———. *More Stories from My Father's Court.* Translated by Curt Leviant. New York,

———. *Nobel Lecture.* New York: Farrar, Straus and Giroux, 1979. Reprinted as "Nobel Lecture, 8 December, 1978." In *Nobel Lectures: Literature, 1968–1980*, edited by Tore Frängsmyr and Sture Allen, 163–65. Singapore: World Scientific Publishing Co., 1993. Audio recording available online at Nobelprize.org, "The Nobel Prize in Literature 1978: Isaac Bashevis Singer; Nobel Lecture, 8 December, 1978." http://nobelprize.org/nobel_prizes/literature/laureates/1978/singer-lecture.html.

———. "On Translating My Books." In *The World of Translation*, 109–14. New York: PEN American Center, 1971.

Slezkine, Yuri. *The Jewish Century.* Princeton, N.J.: Princeton University Press, 2004.

Stanislawski, Michael. "Russia: Russian Empire." In *YIVO Encyclopedia of Jews in Eastern Europe*, edited by Gershon David Hundert. New Haven, Conn.: Yale University Press, 2008. http://www.yivoencyclopedia.org/article.aspx/Russia/Russian_Empire.

Steiner, George. *After Babel: Aspects of Language and Translation*. New York: Oxford University Press, 1975.

Stern, Michael. "Tevye's Art of Quotation." *Prooftexts: A Journal of Jewish Literary History* 6, no. 1 (January 1986): 79–96.

Streisand, Barbra, Jack Rosenthal, and Isaac Bashevis Singer. *Yentl: Screenplay*. N.p., 1981.

Sutzkever, Avrom [Abraham Sutzkever]. Untitled. In *Lider fun togbukh: Poems 1974–1976*, 16. Tel Aviv: Di Goldene Keyt, 1977.

TRANSLATIONS

Harshav, Barbara, and Benjamin Harshav. "Who will remain, what will remain? A wind will stay behind." In *A. Sutzkever: Selected Poetry and Prose*, 33. Berkeley: University of California Press, 1991.

Ozick, Cynthia. Untitled. In *The Penguin Book of Modern Yiddish Verse*, edited by Irving Howe, Ruth R. Wisse, and Chone Shmeruk, 696. New York: Viking, 1987.

Tevye. DVD. Directed by and starring Maurice Schwartz. 1939; Waltham, Mass.: National Center for Jewish Films, 1989.

Trunk, Y. Y. *Tevye un Menakhem Mendl in yidishn veltgoyrl* [Tevye and Menakhem Mendl in Jewish world-destiny]. New York: CYCO, 1944.

Tuvya va-sheva' benotav [Tevye and his seven daughters]. DVD. Directed by Menachem Golan. 1968; [Neve Ilan, Israel]: Globus Group, n.d.

Venuti, Lawrence. Introduction to *The Translation Studies Reader*. 2nd ed. Edited by Lawrence Venuti, 43–63. New York: Routledge, 2004.

Weiner, Meyer. "On Sholem Aleichem's Humor." Translated by Ruth R. Wisse. *Prooftexts: A Journal of Jewish Literary History* 6, no. 1 (January 1986): 41–54.

———. *Tsu der geshikhte fun der yidisher literatur in19tn yorhundert*. [On the history of Yiddish literature in the nineteenth century.] New York: YKUF, 1946.

Weinreich, Max. *The History of the Yiddish Language*. Translated by Shlomo Noble. Chicago: University of Chicago Press, 1980.

Weinreich, Uriel, ed. "Translations of 'Bontshe Shvayg' in English." In *The Field of Yiddish*, vol. 1. New York: Linguistic Circle of New York, 1954.

Whitman, Ruth. "Translating with Isaac Bashevis Singer." In *Critical Views of Isaac Bashevis Singer*, edited by Irving Malin, 44–47. New York: New York University Press, 1969.

Wiener, Leo. *The History of Yiddish Literature in the Nineteenth Century*. New York: Charles Scribner's Sons, 1899.

———, trans. *Songs from the Ghetto*, by Morris Rosenfeld. Boston: Copeland and Day, 1898.

Wisse, Ruth R. *I. L. Peretz and the Making of Modern Jewish Culture*. The Samuel and Althea Stroum Lectures in Jewish Studies. Seattle: University of Washington Press, 1991.

————. "Language as Fate: Reflections on Jewish Literature in America." *Studies in Contemporary Jewry* 12 (1996): 129–47.

————. *The Modern Jewish Canon: A Journey through Language and Culture.* New York: Free Press, 2000.

————. *The Schlemiel as Modern Hero.* Chicago: University of Chicago Press, 1971.

Wolitz, Seth. "The Americanization of Tevye or Boarding the Jewish *Mayflower.*" *American Quarterly* 40, no. 4 (December 1988): 514–36.

Yentl: A Film with Music. VHS. Directed by Barbra Streisand. Screenplay by Jack Rosenthal and Barbra Streisand. 1983; New York: Warner Home Video, 1983.

Zipperstein, Steven J. *Rosenfeld's Lives: Fame, Oblivion, and the Furies of Writing.* New Haven, Conn.: Yale University Press, 2009.

Index

Abel, Hilde, 98, 99
Adam, in Singer's Gimpel story, 50
After Babel (Steiner), 7, 76
aggression and translation, 8, 17
"*A gute nakht, velt*". *See* "Good Night,
World" (Glatshteyn)
Aleichem, Sholem. *See Tevye der
milkhiker* (Sholem Aleichem)
Alfred A. Knopf, 46, 136*n*7
Amalekites, in Glatshteyn's poem, 83
America: in Sholem Aleichem's Tevye
story, 25, 37, 133*n*10; in Singer's Yentl
story, 59, 60
American film version, Sholem
Aleichem's Tevye story. See *Fiddler
on the Roof* (Jewison, director)
"The Americanization of Tevye" (Wolitz),
135*n*31
angels laughing, Peretz's Bontshe story,
97, 98–99
Ani ma'amin, 93, 144*n*19
Anshel character, in Singer's Yentl story,
60–64
anxiety of influence, Bloom's theory, 16
Apter, Emily, 131*n*26
assimilation theme, in film versions
of Sholem Aleichem's Tevye story,
32–34
Astrakhan, Dimitri. See *Get Thee Out*
(Astrakhan, director)
Auden, W. H., 66, 77
audience question, 13–14, 107–8, 130*nn*16–17.

See also "Good Night, World"
(Glatshteyn); Singer, Isaac Bashevis;
Tevye story, film adaptations
Avigdor character, in Singer's Yentl story,
60, 63, 64

Babel, Isaac, 28
"Back to the Ghetto," 71
bahoftn, in Singer's Yentl story, 63
Barnstone, Willis, 15–16, 131*n*22
Bashevis, Yitzhok. *See* Singer, Isaac
Bashevis
Bassnett, Susan, 14
Bell, Daniel, 136*n*8
Bellow, Saul, 46–51, 136*n*8, 137*n*10, *n*14, *n*16
Benjamin, Walter, 5, 13–14, 15, 76, 130*n*16,
143*n*11
Berger, Zackary Sholem (translation of
Glatshteyn's poem): complete poem,
127–28; first stanza elements, 75, 79,
80, 81, 82; publication date, 71; second
stanza elements, 83, 84, 87; third stanza
elements, 90, 92–93, 95
Bernstein, Michael André, 23
betrayal by augment, Steiner's argument,
52
Beylke character, in Sholem Aleichem's
Tevye story, 25, 33–34, 133*n*10
Bible translations, 7–8, 100–101
blaybn translations, from Sutzkever's
poem, 6
Bloom, Harold, 16–17

Blum, Etta (translation of Glatshteyn's poem): complete poem, 120–23; first stanza elements, 74, 79, 81, 82; publication date, 71; second stanza elements, 83, 84, 85, 86, 87, 88; third stanza elements, 89, 90, 92, 93, 95
Bock, Jerome, 28
"Bontshe Shvayg" (Peretz), 97–100
Boyarin, Daniel, 142*n*53
Bruria, 142*n*53
Buchen, Irving, 140*n*33
Burroughs, William, 77

Canby, Vincent, 134*n*17
Carr, Maurice, 54, 139*n*32
census data, Yiddish speakers, 77
Chagall, Marc, 29, 134*n*19
Chava character, in Tevye story: film versions, 32–34, 36, 37, 38; Sholem Aleichem's text, 25, 133*n*10
cheder, 30, 42–43, 57
Chekhov, Anton, 134*n*18
Chicago Jewish Forum, 70
children's literature, Yiddish translations, 11–12
"Chrestomathy" section, in Wiener's *History*, 100–102
Christian references: in Singer's Gimpel story, 50–51, 138*n*19, *nn*23–24; in translations of Glatshteyn's poem, 91–93; Yiddish translations generally, 12, 130*n*12. *See also* holy fool debate
chutzpah, Glatshteyn's poem, 83–84
classical literature, Yiddish translations, 11–12
coming back, in translations of Glatshteyn's poem, 94–95
conversion, in translations of Glatshteyn's poem, 78–80
Corinthians, 49, 137*n*17
cross-dressing, in Singer's Yentl story, 60, 141*n*50
curses, in translations of Glatshteyn's poem, 78–80

daled ames translations, Glatshteyn's poem, 93–94
The Dance of the Demons (Kreitman), 54, 139*n*32
Dawidowicz, Lucy, 136*n*8
daytsh, defined, 9
Deborah, in Krietman's novel, 54–55, 140*n*33
Delos, 76–77, 130*n*16, 143*n*11
de Man, Paul, 13, 129*n*5, 131*n*26
Derrida, Jacques, 131*n*26
Der sotn in goray (Singer), 45
derveyl translation, Molodovsky's poem, 105–6, 145*n*13
destinations, in Sholem Aleichem's Tevye story, 25, 133*n*10
diacritical marks, in Yiddish, 19–20, 88, 105
Di Family Moskat (Singer), 45–46
din translations, Glatshteyn's poem, 87–88, 144*n*18
dolmetcher, defined, 8–9
dolmetchn, defined, 8–9
Dolmetschen, 129*n*6
dos, in Singer's Gimpel story, 50–51, 138*n*23
Drucker, Sally Ann, 137*n*16

Eliot, T. S., 46–47
"El khanun" (Molodovsky), 102–7, 145*nn*13–14
El Malei Rakhamim, 31–32, 39
ending scenes, film versions of Sholem Aleichem's Tevye story, 26, 27, 36–39
enemies, in translations of Glatshteyn's poem, 83, 144*n*16
English film version, Sholem Aleichem's Tevye story. See *Fiddler on the Roof* (Jewison, director)
"Envy" (Ozick), 18, 132*n*31
Evan-Zohar, Itamar, 14
Eve, in Singer's Gimpel story, 50
excommunication, in translations of Glatshteyn's poem, 78–80

Eysteinsson, Astradur, 130*n*16
Ezrahi, Sidra DeKoven, 47

The Family Moskat (Singer), 45–46, 58
family theme, in Sholem Aleichem's
  Tevye story. See *Tevye der milkhiker*
  (Sholem Aleichem); Tevye story, film
  adaptations
Fanon, Frantz, 18
farshemt translations, Peretz's Bontshe
  story, 98–99
fartaytshn, defined, 8–9
fartaytsht un farbesert, 12–13
father, in Singer's memoir, 53
Fein, Richard (translation of Glatshteyn's
  poem): complete poem, 124–25; first
  stanza elements, 75, 79–80, 81, 82;
  publication date, 71; second stanza
  elements, 83, 84, 87–88; third stanza
  elements, 90, 93, 95
Feldshuh, Tovah, 141*n*48
Feuer, Menachem, 137*n*17
Fiddler on the Roof (Jewison, director):
  overview, 27–29, 39–41; Chagall's
  musicians, 29, 134*n*19; Chava's post-
  marriage scene, 33; ending scene,
  37–38, 135*n*31; Japanese adaptations,
  132*n*1; location for, 28, 134*n*13, 135*n*26;
  opening scene, 29–30; pogrom scene,
  34; Topol casting, 135*n*21; *Yentl* com-
  parisons, 59–60
Fishman, Joshua, 77–78
Folk un velt, 71
fool, in Singer's Gimpel story, 48–51,
  137*nn*14–18, 138*n*19
four cubits, in translations of Glatshteyn's
  poem, 93–94
Foverts, 52, 139*n*28
Frank, Helena, 97, 98, 99
free will, in translations of Glatshteyn's
  poem, 72–76
Frye, Northrup, 77
future tense, in Sutzkever's poem, 6
Fyedka character, in film versions of

Sholem Aleichem's Tevye story, 32,
  37, 38

gaonus translation, Molodovsky's
  poem, 106
garbage images, in translations of
  Glatshteyn's poem, 80–82
Garrin, Stephen H., 140*n*40
Gedenklider (Glatshteyn), 82
gender-based exclusion, 42–43
generation-based exclusion, 42–43
geography-based exclusion, 42–43
German language: Benjamin's work, 76,
  130*n*16, 131*n*26, 143*n*11; Singer's translations, 57–58; Wiener's work, 100–
  102; as Yiddish foundation, 8–9,
  129*nn*5–6; Yiddish writers' use, 18
Germans, in Glatshteyn's poem, 83
geshmadte shpurn translations,
  Glatshteyn's poem, 78–80
Get Thee Out (Astrakhan, director),
  27–29, 31–33, 35–36, 38–41, 134*n*17
geyst/gayst, in Margolin's poem, 19–20
ghetto light, in translations of Glatshteyn's
  poem, 84–87
"Gimpel the Fool" (Singer), 46, 47–51,
  137*nn*14–18, 138*n*19, *nn*23–24
Glatshteyn, Yankev: on Singer's reputation, 140*n*40; "Without Jews" poem,
  71. *See also* "Good Night, World"
  (Glatshteyn)
God: in Margolin's poem, 19; in trans-
  lations of Sutzkever's poem, 6
God of Mercy, in Astrakhan's *Get Thee
  Out*, 31–32, 39
"God of Mercy" (Molodovsky), 102–7,
  145*nn*13–14
Golan, Menahem. See *Tevye and His
  Seven Daughters* (Golan, director)
Golde character, in Tevye story: film
  versions, 37, 38; Sholem Aleichem's
  text, 27
The Golden Peacock (Leftwich, ed.), 71
Goldman, Eric, 134*n*12

Goodman, Henry, 97, 99
"Good Night, World" (Glatshteyn): overview, 66–67, 96; author's reading of,
67–69, 88; complete translations,
69–70, 113–27; first stanza translations
compared, 72–76, 78–82; and Jewish
culture growth, 77–78; second stanza
translations compared, 82–88; significance of *Delos* publication, 76–77;
third stanza translations compared,
88–95; translation history summarized, 70–72
Gorky, Maxim, 29, 134*n*18
Gottlieb, Elaine, 139*n*28
goyim, in Singer's Gimpel story, 50
grammar structure, in translations:
Glatshteyn's poem, 84–85; Sutzkever's
poem, 6
Greenberg, Eliezer, 51, 138*n*24
Gross, A. H., 136*n*4
Grossman, Anita Susan, 136*n*5

Hadass character, in Singer's Yentl story,
60–63
Hadda, Janet, 46, 50, 51, 137*n*18, 138*n*19
Haiblum, Isidore, 136*n*7
Halkin, Hillel, 98, 99
Hamburger, Michael, 77
Hamsun, Knut, 57
Harshav, Barbara and Benjamin (transla-
tion of Sutzkever poem), 4–5, 6–7
Harshav, Benjamin, on semiotics of
Yiddish, 11
Harshav, Benjamin and Barbara (trans-
lation of Glatshteyn's poem): complete
poem, 69–70, 123–24; first stanza ele-
ments, 74–75, 79, 81, 82; second stanza
elements, 83, 144*n*16; third stanza ele-
ments, 94
Havdalah service scene, in Schwartz's
Tevye, 32–33
Hebrew film version, Sholem Aleichem's
Tevye story, 27–29, 30–31, 33, 34–35,
38, 39–41

Hebrew language, 8, 18, 39, 78, 100–101,
106
Hellerstein, Kathryn, 19, 110, 145*nn*13–14
"Hello" experience, author's, ix–x
heymish, Singer's English, 53
"Hi" experience, author's, ix–x
*History of Yiddish Literature in the
Nineteenth Century* (Wiener), 100–
102
Hodl character, in Sholem Aleichem's
Tevye story, 25, 133*n*10
Holocaust: and Bellow's Prufrock translation, 47–48; and Jewish culture
growth, 77–78, 96; and Peretz's Bontshe story, 100; and Sholem Aleichem's
characters, 18, 34, 37; and translation
practices, 9–10, 43, 107
holy fool debate, Singer's Gimpel story,
49–50, 51, 137*n*17, 138*n*19
hope, in translations of Glatshteyn's
poem, 91–93
hot zikh tselakht translations, Peretz's
Bontshe story, 98–99
Howe, Irving, 51, 57, 104–7
Howells, William Dean, 102
hunchback, in translations of Glatshteyn's
poem, 80–82, 87
Hynd, James, 76, 130*n*16

ibertsuraysn, in Singer's Yentl story, 63
iberzetsung, etymological connections, 8,
9
Ibn Tibbon, Samuel, 15
"Illuminations" (Benjamin), 143*n*11
impossibility of translation accuracy, 16,
43–44, 131*n*26
In My Father's Court (Singer), 52,
139*nn*28–29
Inzikh, 82
inzikhistn, 67
An Isaac Bashevis Singer Reader (Singer),
139*n*29
Israel, in Sholem Aleichem's Tevye story,
25, 133*n*10

Jacobs, Carol, 13
Japanese adaptation, *Fiddler on the Roof,*
  132*n*1
Jesus, in Singer's Gimpel story, 50–51,
  138*nn*23–24
Jesusmarxes, in translations of Glatshteyn's
  poem, 88–91
Jewison, Norman, on his heritage, 134*n*16.
  See also *Fiddler on the Roof* (Jewison,
  director)
Job, 23–24, 98, 138*n*19

Katz, Eli, 98, 99
Keats, John, 16, 131*n*28
Kermode, Frank, 77
kheyrem translations, Glatshteyn's poem,
  78–80
Kh'tu dermonen (Glatshteyn), 82
Kleinerman-Goldstein, Channah, 139*n*28
Knopf, Alfred A., 46, 136*n*7
krapir translations, Glatshteyn's poem,
  88–91
Kreitman, Esther Singer, 44, 53–55, 139*n*32,
  140*n*33
Kresh, Paul, 141*n*47
kumen translations, Glatshteyn's poem,
  94–95
Kumove, Shirley, 19, 111
Kuprin, Aleksandr, 28, 134*n*18

Landis, Joseph C., 138*n*19
"Language as Fate" (Wisse), 136*n*8
laughter of angels, Peretz's Bontshe story,
  97, 98–99
law, in translations of Glatshteyn's poem,
  87–88, 144*n*18
Lebensboym, Rosa. *See* Margolin, Anna
Leftwich, Joseph (translation of
  Glatshteyn's poem): complete poem,
  113–14; cultural significance, 70, 71–72;
  first stanza elements, 72–73, 74, 79, 80,
  82; second stanza elements, 83; third
  stanza elements, 89, 90–91, 93, 95
Leviant, Curt, 139*n*29

liberators, in translations of Glatshteyn's
  poem, 88–91
Lider fun togbukh (Sutzkever), 3–7
The Literature of Destruction (Roskies,
  ed.), 144*n*18
"The Love Song of J. Alfred Prufrock"
  (Eliot), 46–47, 136*n*8, 137*n*10
Lowell, Robert, 77
loyb phrase, in Glatshteyn's poem, 80–82

Maimonides, 15, 93, 144*n*19
Manseau, Peter, 13
Margolin, Anna, 19–20, 109–11
"Maris tfile" (Margolin), 19–20, 109–11
marriage portrayals, in Sholem Aleichem's
  Tevye story, 25
"Mary's Prayer" (Margolin), 19–20, 109–11
Mayn tatns bezdn-shtub (Singer), 139*n*28
Menakhem Mendl character, in Sholem
  Aleichem's Tevye story, 25
Mendelssohn, Moses, 100–101
Mendl character, in Sholem Aleichem's
  Tevye story, 25
messiah, in translations of Glatshteyn's
  poem, 91–93
MetroCard languages, 130*n*7
meyn translations, Glatshteyn's poem,
  84–87, 88
Miron, Dan, 135*n*25
Molodovsky, Kadya, "El khanun" poem,
  102–7, 145*nn*13–14
money, in Sholem Aleichem's Tevye story,
  25, 30–31
mother, Singer's, 53–54
Motl character, in Astrakhan's *Get Thee
  Out,* 32, 33–34, 35–36, 37, 39
mourning scenes, in film versions of
  Sholem Aleichem's Tevye story, 32–33
multilingualism, Yiddish writers, 18

Nabokov, Vladimir, viii
Nachman of Bratslav, 48–49, 137*n*15
Naomi, in Book of Ruth, 36
nar, in Singer's Gimpl story, 48–49

National Jewish Monthly, 58
negative capability, Keats' theory, 16,
    131n28
Nehemiah, Book of, 7
New York City, subway station languages,
    130n7
New Yorker, 13
New York Times, 59
nisht geshtoygn, nisht gefloygn, 13, 51,
    130n12
nonkosher cultures, in translations
    of Glatshteyn's poem, 78–80

"On Translating 'Eugene Onegin'
    (Nabokov), viii
opening scenes, in film versions of
    Sholem Aleichem's Tevye story,
    29–32
Operation Shylock (Roth), 47
"orders are orders" theme, in film
    versions of Sholem Aleichem's Tevye
    story, 34, 35
Ozick, Cynthia, 4–5, 6–7, 18, 132n31

Palestine, in Sholem Aleichem's Tevye
    story, 25, 133n10
Partisan Review, 47
pasekh, 19, 88, 105
paternal pride theme, in Sholem
    Aleichem's Tevye story, 25
Peretz, I. L., "Bontshe Shvayg" story,
    97–100
Poggioli, Renato, 16
pogroms, in Singer's fiction, 45
pogroms, in Tevye story: English film,
    34, 134n13, 135n26; Hebrew film, 30,
    34–35; Russian film, 31–32, 35–36,
    38–39; Sholem Aleichem's text, 26,
    34; Yiddish film, 34
Poles, in Glatshteyn's poem, 83
Pope, Alexander, 22
population statistics, Russian Jews,
    135n23

"The Position of Translated Literature
    within the Literary Polysystem"
    (Evan-Zohar), 14
possessive pronouns, Glatshteyn's poem,
    94
postvernacular Yiddish, 11
preservation perspective of Yiddish
    language, 43
profundity, in translations of Glatshteyn's
    poem, 88, 144n18
pronouns, in Singer's Yentl story, 60–62
Prooftexts (Stern), 133n7
punctuation placement, in Glatshteyn's
    poem, 80–82, 84–85
pupik image, 46–47, 136n8

quotations, in Sholem Aleichem's Tevye
    story, 25, 133n7

Rabbi Yehuda, 9
Rabinovitch, Motl Salomnovitch, 32,
    33–34
Raphael, Chaim, 136n8
reader response theories, 15–16
redeemer, in translations of Glatshteyn's
    poem, 91–93
Renoir, Alain, 143n9
resistance perspective, translating
    Yiddish, 43
The Resistance to Theory (de Man),
    129n5
return. See "Good Night, World"
    (Glatshteyn)
Rosenfeld, Isaac, 46–47, 136n8, 137n10
Rosenfeld, Morris, 102
Rosenwald, Lawrence, 19, 110
Roskies, David, 137n15, 144n18
Roth, Philip, 47
Rumanians, in translation of Glatshteyn's
    poem, 83
Russia, in Sholem Aleichem's Tevye story,
    25, 133n10
Russian film version, Sholem Aleichem's

Tevye story, 27–29, 31–33, 35–36, 38–41, 134*n*17
Ruth, Book of, 36

Samuel, Maurice, 97, 99, 136*n*4
Saposnik, Irving, 46
Sapozhikov, Gershom, 138*n*19
Satan in Goray (Singer), 45
Schleiermacher, Friedrich, 3, 129*n*6
Schmitz, Andrew, 137*n*17
Schwartz, Maurice. See *Tevye* (Schwartz, director)
Seidman, Naomi, 7, 50, 138*nn*23–24, 141*n*50
Septuagint, 7–8
Shakespeare, adaptation myth, 12–13
Shandler, Jeffrey, 11, 130*nn*7–8, 132*n*31
Der sheydim tants (Kreitman), 54, 139*n*32, 140*n*33
shiksas, in Singer's Gimpel story, 50
"Der shir hashirim fun Mendl Pumshtok" (Bellow and Rosenfeld), 46–47, 136*n*8, 137*n*10
shkineh translation, Molodovsky's poem, 106
shlepping golus, 37
shlimazl character, in Sholem Aleichem's Tevye story, 25
Shmeruk, Chone, 48
Sholem Aleichem. See *Tevye der milkhiker* (Sholem Aleichem)
Shprintse character, in Sholem Aleichem's Tevye story, 25
shtetl life, 11, 42–43. See also *Tevye der milkhiker* (Sholem Aleichem); Tevye story, film adaptations
silence theme, in Peretz's Bontshe story, 97–100
Singer, Isaac Bashevis: audience question, 42, 136*n*5; background, 44–45; dismissal of scholars, 52, 139*n*27; language treatments, 45, 51–52, 136*n*4, 139*n*29; Nobel Prize presentation, 55–57,

140*n*36; reputation of, 44, 55, 77, 140*n*40; role in translation process, 45, 57–58, 140*n*33; translation skills, 57–58, 140*n*41; on writing for the reader, 57; YIVO event, 43–44
Singer, Isaac Bashevis (works by): *The Family Moskat*, 45–46, 58, 136*n*4; "Gimpel the Fool," 46, 47–51, 137*nn*14–18, 138*n*19, *nn*23–24; *An Isaac Bashevis Singer Reader*, 139*n*29; *In My Father's Court*, 52, 139*nn*28–29; *Satan in Goray*, 45; "Yentl der yeshive-bokher," 58–65, 141*nn*47–48, *n*50
Singer, Israel Joshua, 44
Singer, Joseph, 139*n*28
Slezkine, Yuri, 133*n*10
"The Song of Songs of Mendl Pumshtok" (Bellow and Rosenfeld), 46–47, 136*n*8, 137*n*10
Songs from the Ghetto (Wiener, ed.), 102
Spiegel, Moshe (translation of Glatshteyn's poem): complete poem, 114–15; first stanza elements, 73, 74, 79, 80, 82; publication history, 70; second stanza elements, 83, 84, 85, 87–88; third stanza elements, 89, 90, 91, 92, 93, 95
Spiegel, Moshe (translation of Peretz's Bontshe story), 98, 99
Stanislawski, Michael, 13
"The State of Translation" (in *Delos*), 77
Stein, Joseph, 28
Stein, Norman, 132*n*1
Steiner, George, 7, 16, 51–52, 76
Stern, Isaac, 134*n*19
Stern, Michael, 133*n*7
Streisand, Barbra, 58–64, 141*n*48
subway station languages, 130*n*7
Sutzkever, Avrom: on *derveyl* meaning, 145*n*13; *Lider fun togbukh* poem, 3–7, 21, 108
s'yoyzel, in Singer's Gimpel story, 50–51, 138*n*23

Syrkin, Marie (translation of Glatshteyn's poem): complete poem, 117–20; first stanza elements, 73, 74, 79, 81, 82; publication date, 71; second stanza elements, 83, 84, 85, 87, 88; third stanza elements, 89, 92, 93

tam: in Singer's Gimpel story, 48–51, 137*nn*14–17, 138*n*19; translation loss worries, 9

"The Task of the Translator" (Benjamin), 13–14, 76, 130*n*16, 143*n*11

taytsh, defined, 9

Tevya und seine Töchter (German film), 134*n*15

Tevye and His Seven Daughters (Golan, director), 27–29, 30–31, 33, 34–35, 38, 39–41

Tevye der milkhiker (Sholem Aleichem): adaptation popularity, 22–23, 27, 132*n*1; character-author similarities, 31, 135*n*25; ending scene, 26, 36–37; money portrayal, 25, 30–31; narrator perspective, 132*n*3; pogrom portrayals, 34, 35; Russian history context, 26–27, 135*n*23; themes summarized, 23–24, 25; writing of, 24–26, 133*n*6

Tevye (Schwartz, director), 27–29, 32–33, 34, 36–37, 39–41, 134*n*12

Tevye story, film adaptations: overview, 27–29, 39–41; Hebrew version, 30–31, 33, 34–35, 38, 39–41; Russian version, 31–33, 35–36, 38–41, 134*n*17; Yiddish version, 32–33, 34, 36–37, 134*n*12. See also *Fiddler on the Roof* (Jewison, director)

three Gs of Yiddish scholarship, 42–43

Tom comparison, Singer's Gimpel, 137*n*17

Topol, Chaim, 30, 134*n*13, 135*n*21

tradition portrayals, in Jewison's *Fiddler on the Roof,* 29–30

transgression and translation, 8, 65, 66

translation practices, overview: anxieties about, 7–10; audience question, 13–16, 107–8, 130*nn*16–17; cultural problem, 17–18; culture value, 10–12, 16; impossibility perspective, 16, 131*n*26; interpretation accusations, 12–14; latent structure task, 14–15, 131*n*21; mediation challenges, 16–17; necessity argument, 5–7; obsolescence pattern, 143*n*9; as ongoing conversation, 20–21; spatial/perceptual problem, 18–19

Translation—Theory and Practice (Weissbort and Eysteinsson), 130*n*16

treyfene kulturn translations, Glatshteyn's poem, 78–80

Trilling, Lionel, 77

Tsaytl character, in Sholem Aleichem's Tevye story: film versions, 34, 36; original text, 25

tsum tifn meyn translations, Glatshteyn's poem, 84–87, 88

tsurik translations, Glatshteyn's poem, 84–85

tsushtayer translations, Glatshteyn's poem, 88–91

übersetzen, etymological connections, 8, 129*n*5

Valk, E. M., 76, 130*n*16

Venuti, Lawrence, 14

virginity, in Singer's Yentl story, 61–63

vor, in Singer's Gimpel story, 49–50

wedding night, in Singer's Yentl story, 62–63

Weiner, Meyer, 40

Weinreich, Max, 18

Weissbort, Daniel, 130*n*16

Whitman, Ruth (translation of Glatshteyn's poem): overview, 71, 72; complete poem, 115–17; first stanza elements, 73, 74, 76, 79, 80, 82; second stanza elements, 83, 84, 85, 88; third stanza elements, 90–91, 93, 95

Wiener, Leo, 97, 99, 100–102, 145*n*7

Wiener, Norbert, 145*n*7

Wisse, Ruth R., 47, 132*n*3, 136*n*8, 137*n*10, *n*14, *n*18

"Without Jews" (Glatshteyn), 71

Wolitz, Seth, 132*n*1, 135*n*31

World Jewish Congress, 71

World Jewry, 71, 83

Yehuda, Rabbi, 9

Yente character, in Jewison's *Fiddler on the Roof*, 135*n*31

"Yentl der yeshive-bokher" (Singer), 58–65, 141*n*47, *n*50

Yentl (Streisand's movie), 57–64, 141*n*48

yeshiva, 42–43. See also Yentl *entries*

Yiddish film version, Sholem Aleichem's Tevye story, 27–29, 32–33, 34, 36–37, 134*n*12

Yiddish language, overview: census data, 77; three Gs proclamation, 42–43, 44. See also specific topics, e.g., *Fiddler on the Roof*; Singer, Isaac Bashevis; translation practices, overview

Yiddish transliterations: diacritical marking example, 19; Glatshteyn's poem, 67–69; Margolin's poem, 109; Molodovsky's poem, 102–3; Peretz's Bontshe story, 98; Sholem Aleichem's chapter titles, 24; Singer's Nobel Prize presentation, 55–56; Singer's Yentl story, 61, 63; Sutzkever's poem, 3–4

Yidisher Kemfer, 47

YIVO event, Singer's reading, 43–44

Yoyzl, in Singer's Gimpel story, 50–51, 138*n*23

Zohn, Harry, 130*n*16, 131*n*21, 143*n*11

Zumoff, Barnett (translation of Glatshteyn's poem): complete poem, 125–27; first stanza elements, 75, 79, 81, 82; publication date, 71; second stanza elements, 83, 84, 86–87, 88; third stanza elements, 90, 92, 93, 95

Zynger, Hinde Ester, 44, 53–54, 139*n*32, 140*n*33

Zynger, Moshe, 44

Zynger, Yisroel, 44

Zynger, Yitzhok Hersh. *See* Singer, Isaac Bashevis

THE SAMUEL & ALTHEA STROUM
LECTURES IN JEWISH STUDIES

The Yiddish Art Song
performed by Leon Lishner, basso, and Lazar Weiner, piano (stereophonic record album)

The Holocaust in Historical Perspective
Yehuda Bauer

Zakhor: Jewish History and Jewish Memory
Yosef Hayim Yerushalmi

Jewish Mysticism and Jewish Ethics
Joseph Dan

The Invention of Hebrew Prose: Modern Fiction and the Language of Realism
Robert Alter

Recent Archaeological Discoveries and Biblical Research
William G. Dever

Jewish Identity in the Modern World
Michael A. Meyer

I. L. Peretz and the Making of Modern Jewish Culture
Ruth R. Wisse

The Kiss of God: Spiritual and Mystical Death in Judaism
Michael Fishbane

Gender and Assimilation in Modern Jewish History:
The Roles and Representation of Women
Paula E. Hyman

Portrait of American Jews: The Last Half of the 20th Century
Samuel C. Heilman

Judaism and Hellenism in Antiquity: Conflict or Confluence?
Lee I. Levine

Imagining Russian Jewry: Memory, History, Identity
Steven J. Zipperstein

Popular Culture and the Shaping of Holocaust Memory in America
Alan Mintz

Studying the Jewish Future
Calvin Goldscheider

Autobiographical Jews: Essays in Jewish Self-Fashioning
Michael Stanislawski

The Jewish Life Cycle: Rites of Passage from Biblical to Modern Times
Ivan Marcus

Make Yourself a Teacher: Rabbinic Tales of Mentors and Disciples
Susan Handelman

Writing in Tongues: Translating Yiddish in the Twentieth Century
Anita Norich

Agnon's Moonstruck Lovers: The Song of Songs in Israeli Culture
Ilana Pardes